Professional Writing

Lisa Kesteven • Andrew Melrose
# Professional Writing
## Creative and Critical Approaches

Lisa Kesteven  
Chilbolton, Hampshire, UK

Andrew Melrose  
Brighton, UK

ISBN 978-3-030-84898-9     ISBN 978-3-030-84899-6   (eBook)
https://doi.org/10.1007/978-3-030-84899-6

© The Editor(s) (if applicable) and The Author(s), under exclusive licence to Springer Nature Switzerland AG 2022
This work is subject to copyright. All rights are solely and exclusively licensed by the Publisher, whether the whole or part of the material is concerned, specifically the rights of translation, reprinting, reuse of illustrations, recitation, broadcasting, reproduction on microfilms or in any other physical way, and transmission or information storage and retrieval, electronic adaptation, computer software, or by similar or dissimilar methodology now known or hereafter developed.
The use of general descriptive names, registered names, trademarks, service marks, etc. in this publication does not imply, even in the absence of a specific statement, that such names are exempt from the relevant protective laws and regulations and therefore free for general use.
The publisher, the authors and the editors are safe to assume that the advice and information in this book are believed to be true and accurate at the date of publication. Neither the publisher nor the authors or the editors give a warranty, expressed or implied, with respect to the material contained herein or for any errors or omissions that may have been made. The publisher remains neutral with regard to jurisdictional claims in published maps and institutional affiliations.

Cover design: eStudioCalamar

This Palgrave Macmillan imprint is published by the registered company Springer Nature Switzerland AG.
The registered company address is: Gewerbestrasse 11, 6330 Cham, Switzerland

*Professional Writing*
*Andrew Melrose and Lisa Kesteven*
*© 2021*
*We would like to dedicate this book to:*
*(LK) My parents, Tony and Ruth Kesteven*
*(AM) Diane, Abbi and Daniel Melrose*

# Contents

| | | |
|---|---|---|
| **1** | **Introduction to Professional Writing** | 1 |
| | What Is Professional Writing? | 5 |
| |    Can Writing Really Be a Profession? | 6 |
| |    This Book Approaches Professional Writing from These Three Perspectives | 8 |
| | Why Is Professional Writing Critical to Business? | 9 |
| |    What Are Some of the Causes of Poor Professional Writing? | 10 |
| | How Is Professional Writing Different to Other Forms of Writing? | 11 |
| |    Lose Your Own Voice and Become an Imitator! | 11 |
| |    Write to Specification | 12 |
| |    It May Be on a Subject You Don't Know Much About or Have Very Little Interest In | 12 |
| |    It's Professional | 12 |
| | The Demand for High-Quality Content and Copy | 13 |
| | Business Style and a Consistent Image | 14 |
| | Key Chapter Points | 14 |
| **2** | **Writing for Business** | 17 |
| | External Communication | 20 |
| | Internal Communication | 21 |
| | Business Language and Tone | 22 |
| |    How We Communicate Creates an Image | 22 |
| |    Identifying the Subject, Audience and Objective | 24 |
| |    Reader-Friendly Writing and Readability | 25 |

|     | Sentence Structure and Word Choice | 25 |
| --- | --- | --- |
|     | Engaging with Readers | 26 |
|     | The Way of Communication | 26 |
|     | Pressure to Stay in Touch | 26 |
|     | It's All About Image | 26 |
|     | Writing Professionally and the Freelancer | 27 |
|     | The Professional Freelancer … | 27 |
|     | Key Chapter Points | 28 |
| 3   | **A Career in Professional Writing** | 31 |
|     | Writing as a Profession in Business | 31 |
|     | Jobs Available to Professional Writers | 33 |
|     | Turning Your Written Words into a Paying Proposition | 38 |
|     | The Life of a Freelance Writer | 43 |
|     | Standing Out from the Crowd | 46 |
|     | Key Chapter Points | 47 |
| 4   | **The Art of Communication and the Freelancer** | 49 |
|     | The Freelance Writer and Communication | 50 |
|     | How Does Communicating Professionally and Business-like Differ from Other Forms of Communication? | 52 |
|     | Getting Your Message Across | 54 |
|     | Use Active Voice | 54 |
|     | Avoid Passive Voice | 54 |
|     | Stick to Simple and Shorter Sentence Structures | 54 |
|     | Be Specific | 55 |
|     | Be Positive But Curb Enthusiasm | 55 |
|     | Avoid Qualifiers | 55 |
|     | Keep It Professional at All Times | 55 |
|     | Write from the Point of View of the Company | 55 |
|     | Write More Univocally | 55 |
|     | Avoid Nominalising Verbs | 56 |
|     | Recommend Action Rather Than Refer to Individual Mental States | 56 |
|     | Avoid Qualifiers That Weaken Recommendations Or Express Doubt | 56 |
|     | Avoid Personalising Pronouns, and Personalising Problems | 56 |
|     | Use the Imperative Voice | 56 |

|   |   |
|---|---|
| Use Verbal Rather Than Nominal Forms (Verbs Changed into Nouns Or Adjectives) of Words | 57 |
| Use Parallel Structure | 57 |
| Eliminate Unnecessary Words | 57 |
| Select Words in an Appropriate Register (Vocabulary and Tone) for Your Reader | 58 |
| Provide Possible Solutions and Any Implications | 58 |
| Be Cautious with the Use of Jargon | 58 |
| The Humble Email | 58 |
|   Emailing for Success | 59 |
|   General Email Etiquette | 60 |
|   Addressing an Email | 60 |
|   Subject Line | 61 |
|   Body of the Email | 61 |
|   Some Examples | 62 |
|   Why Is This Better? | 63 |
|   Bad Email Habits | 64 |
|   Good Email Habits | 64 |
|   Disclaimers | 65 |
|   Signatures | 65 |
| Key Chapter Points | 65 |

## 5 Writing for an Online Market — 69

|   |   |
|---|---|
| Writing for Digital Media | 70 |
| The Style Guide | 72 |
| Digital Platform Choice | 73 |
| Creating Scannable Content | 74 |
|   Copy People Want to Read! | 76 |
|   The Visual and Verbal, Alongside the Written | 78 |
| Assessing and Evaluating Online Copy | 79 |
| Key Chapter Points | 79 |

## 6 Self-promotion — 83

|   |   |
|---|---|
| Becoming an Expert Self-marketeer | 84 |
|   Have a Website Dedicated to Your Freelancing Writing | 85 |
|   Blogs | 86 |
|   Forums | 87 |
| What Are You Good At? | 87 |

## Contents

|   |   |
|---|---|
| Identifying Your Strengths and Weaknesses | 87 |
| A Standout Profile | 88 |
| Making Your Profile Stand Out | 90 |
| The Freelance Writer's Portfolio | 90 |
| Change Your Portfolio Regularly | 91 |
| Refresh Your Content | 92 |
| Portfolio Content | 92 |
| Key Chapter Points | 95 |

### 7 Finding Work — 97

|   |   |
|---|---|
| Finding Work | 98 |
| Traditional Sources to Find Writing Gigs | 98 |
| Online Sources to Find Writing Gigs | 101 |
| Engaging in Networks | 105 |
| Building Customer Relationships | 106 |
| Creating a Freelancer's CV | 108 |
| CV Style | 108 |
| Profile | 109 |
| Skills List | 109 |
| CV Highlights | 110 |
| Other Sections | 111 |
| Building Your Elevator Pitch | 111 |
| Key Chapter Points | 112 |

### 8 Navigating the Bid Process on Freelancing Platforms — 113

|   |   |
|---|---|
| Freelancing Platforms: How Do They Work? | 113 |
| Identifying Suitable Opportunities | 114 |
| Writing Successful Bid Responses/Proposals | 116 |
| Read the Project Description: And Then Read It Again | 116 |
| Make an Impression | 117 |
| Sell Your Specific Strengths | 117 |
| Details of Your Proposal | 118 |
| Personalise Your Bid | 118 |
| Answer Any Questions | 119 |
| Provide Estimates | 119 |
| Be Polite | 119 |
| Supporting Your Proposal | 120 |
| The Price | 120 |

|  |  |  |
|---|---|---|
| | Your Questions | 120 |
| | Show Your Experience | 121 |
| | Be Clear with What You Will Provide | 121 |
| | Manage Expectations | 121 |
| | Proposal Outline | 122 |
| | Getting Your Proposal Noticed | 122 |
| | You've Won the Bid: Now What? | 123 |
| | Key Chapter Points | 124 |
| **9** | **Estimating Writing Projects** | **127** |
| | Estimating Rate and Work Effort | 127 |
| | Your Basic Rate | 129 |
| | Pricing Your Services | 131 |
| | Price per Project | 131 |
| | Price per Hour | 132 |
| | Price per Word/Page | 133 |
| | Calculating Rates | 133 |
| | The Marketplace | 133 |
| | Know Your Value | 134 |
| | Other Benefits? | 134 |
| | What to Charge? | 135 |
| | Negotiating | 136 |
| | Scoping the Work | 136 |
| | Have Some Standard Guides | 136 |
| | Pricing a Job | 137 |
| | Going Under Your Base Rate? | 137 |
| | Retainers | 138 |
| | Rates Are Not Set in Stone | 138 |
| | Getting Better at Estimating | 138 |
| | Some Useful Guides | 139 |
| | Key Chapter Points | 139 |
| **10** | **Planning and Managing Writing Projects** | **141** |
| | Planning Writing Projects | 141 |
| | Planning Process | 144 |
| | Getting Started: Identify the What, Who, Why and How | 144 |
| | Step-by-Step Planning for Writing Projects | 146 |

## Contents

| | |
|---|---|
| Discussions | 146 |
| Keeping Track of Project Information | 147 |
|     For Each Client | 147 |
|     For Each Project | 148 |
|     For Each Task | 148 |
| Project Management and Writing Projects | 148 |
|     Asengana | 149 |
|     Basecamp | 149 |
|     Evernote | 149 |
|     FreshBooks | 149 |
|     Podio | 150 |
|     Redbooth | 150 |
|     Taskboard | 150 |
|     Thrive | 150 |
|     Trello | 150 |
|     Ulysses III | 150 |
|     Wrike | 151 |
|     Do You Really Need a Fancy Tool? | 151 |
| Key Chapter Points | 151 |

**11 The Editing Process** — 153

| | |
|---|---|
| Thinking About Ways to Edit | 154 |
| Narrative Voice | 156 |
| Negative Positive or Should That Be Positive Negative? | 157 |
| Active Voice | 158 |
| I Would Like To | 158 |
| Punctuation | 159 |
| Word Smart | 160 |
| 'Out of Work' Words | 161 |
| Muscular Verbs | 162 |
| Who, What, Not That, What Not | 163 |
| Currently, Presently, Truly, Deeply—And Killing the—Lys and—Ings | 163 |
| Informal Contractions | 164 |
| Your Little Word and Phrase Tics | 164 |
| Tools to Help with Editing | 164 |
| Key Chapter Points | 166 |

| | | |
|---|---|---|
| **12** | **Building a Successful Career as a Professional Writer** | 167 |
| | Understanding Your Skills and Capabilities | 168 |
| |     Have a Niche or Two … or Three … or Four … | 169 |
| |     Learn, Learn, Learn | 170 |
| | Having Long-Term and Short-Term Career Plans | 173 |
| | When Things Go Wrong | 174 |
| | Key Chapter Points | 175 |

**Appendix: LGA-Banned Words**     177

**Index**     183

# 1

# Introduction to Professional Writing

In this chapter we will:

1. Explore exactly we mean by the term professional writing and its relationship with creative writing.
2. Discuss why professional writing relies on creative writing and why this is important.
3. Discuss why professional writing matters, not just to a writer but to their customers as well.
4. Consider that everything should be written well, so isn't everything technically 'professional writing'? There are some key differences—so even though you'll hopefully always produce quality writing—when you're writing professionally, you'll need to be able deliver top rate work consistently.
5. Consider whether there a demand for writers in this technical age, when everyone has access to software and design applications.
6. Cover what a business style is and why it's essential you get this right for each and every client.

*I'm a writer!*
*I want to be a writer!*
*I could be a writer!*
*I could write that!*

What order should these points be in? And while we are thinking about order, looking at the options, what kind of writer do you want to be? Put them in number order of your preference:

*Poet*
*Novelist*
*Satirist*
*Journalist*
*Blogger*
*Report writer*
*Short story writer*
*Librettist*
*Lyricist*
*Playwright*
*Screenwriter*
*Any others?*

And what kind of writing:

*Creative writing*
*Descriptive writing*
*Expository writing*
*Narrative writing*
*Objective writing*
*Persuasive writing*
*Reviewing*
*Subjective writing*
*Expressive writing*
*Professional writing*
*Blogs*
*Reports*
*Any others?*

Lisa's preferred writing is historical fiction—she is a novelist, but she also writes for children, short stories, journal articles, magazine articles, poetry and a blog. She also has a background in IT and business, and she's written reports and technical documents. Andrew has written films, songs, books of fiction and non-fiction, book chapters, journal articles, magazine articles, poems, chapbooks and a blog. Neither are tied to genre and consistently cross writing genres, categories, classifications and varieties. 'Oh, you're a writer,' we have all heard people say. 'Can I read your novel/poetry …' and so on is the common response to announcing yourself as a writer. And what comes with the announcement or acknowledgement that you are a writer or an author (if you prefer) is the romantic image it conjures up. Most writers would admit to this a little. Mostly because the creative writer is a member of the arts and all that comes with being an artist. Nevertheless, at the bottom of the list is *professional writing* and the image this conjures up. The writer who writes for money. In truth, we would probably all like to make a living out of writing, but sometimes this does mean the 'creative' aspect has to be compromised in some way.

It doesn't take much effort to see that writers not only write 'professionally' as routine but are often seen taking paid writing work which isn't actually what they might 'prefer' to be writing. Often, this is out of sheer economic necessity. Writers make a living out of writing and sometimes this might mean taking 'writing jobs' simply to pay the bills. But who better to take on paid writing than creative writers? For it is they who bring that creative spark to the professional job itself and at no time would any 'professional writer' lose that creative spark. It is what you will be paid for. Your sense of pace, rhythm, rhyme, storytelling … they are all important in the paid writing job. A writer is a wordsmith; their job is to forge the words appropriately for the job. After all, you wouldn't shoe a horse with rubber nails, now would you?

Writing is probably one of the most important developments in communication mankind ever invented. Word-of-mouth knowledge soon became knowledge transcribed on papyrus, stone and anything else we could use to hand down, generation by generation. Bees have been present in human history for over 6000 years and we know how to get their honey without stinging ourselves because someone already wrote down telling us how.

This picture may not look like writing, but it is a means of communication. In this twentieth-first century of ours, though, writing is a huge business and we have moved on a great deal. If you want to be part of it, you need to consider whether you are ready along with another major consideration—which is, can you afford to be a writer? This is where we come in. This isn't a book about writing novels or poetry. It isn't about writing the next Oscar-nominated screenplay. It's about being a professional writer in a professional world and being able to support yourself while your magnum opus is taking shape. Furthermore, this is a book for creative writers because it is our belief that creative writing is very much part of the professional writer's toolbox—the professional writer needs the creative energy of a creative writer.

We also want to reject the idea, upfront, that professional writing is something we only do because it brings in the money until we make it as a poet or fictional author or playwright or whatever. Actually, professional writing can be extremely rewarding. We've found it a great way to add variety to our writing careers, to experiment with different forms and to improve on our writing and written communication.

A Twitter exchange in 2012 between Hari Kunzru (@harikunzru) and Salman Rushdie said,

> The internets [*sic*] allege @salmanrushdie is the is the lyricist for this fine Burnley building society advert from the 1970's. … Salman Rushdie (@salmanrushdie) replied, 'I admit, @harikunzru, that it's true, I did that. I also coined "Adorabubble" for Aero chocolate and called cream cakes "Naughty but nice."' (https://twitter.com/salmanrushdie/status/228557610176106496)

It is nice being able to share this teasing exchange between two critically acclaimed literary figures but what it reveals is that prior to being the Booker Prize–winning writer he went on to become, Rushdie was using his creativity and creative writing skills to earn money by writing advertising copy, which allowed him to write his first novel.

The simple fact is the creative part of writing has a huge and important part to play in the world of professional writing. Look around at examples of professional writing. How often have you seen a website or an article which was so badly written you just turned away from it? Sometimes it's like listening to a bad covers band standing in for your favourite artists. The fact that they are a parody is bad enough, but when they come to do an original song in the style of Bruce Springsteen, Madonna, Iggy Pop or Beyoncé, you just know it's going to be a disaster, and it usually is because it is a parody, a caricature, an imitation and not an originally created idea from the artist. Writers write and important to writing is the edge, the creative spark they bring with them.

Nobody would ask me to bake their wedding cake or paint a mural on their ceiling (at least they shouldn't), so why would anyone expect good copy from someone who isn't a writer?

There is poetry in good copy. 'Naughty but nice' or 'Adorabubble' may not speak of Pablo Neruda, who wrote, 'Love is so short, forgetting is so long…' But is there not a simplicity in expression and delivery which brings the loveliness of the poetry with it? The poem this quotation is from is 'Tonight I Can Write (the Saddest Lines)'. But think about this idea. How does the poet manage to convey emotion? Neruda does this in eight simple words. Ask yourself this, 'can I achieve this in my creative writing and if so can I do it in my professional writing?' Because this poem persuades me. Eight words used to describe a timeless truism, 'Love is so short, forgetting is so long….'

We could go on with this idea; novelists choose their words carefully too, in order to tell a story. We have gone past the idea that any old words are good for storytelling. We enjoy metaphor, alliteration, enjambment, similes, even the playfulness of wordplay. Nothing rhymes with orange, so why would anyone try? Go on, re-arrange it; I could make it a short poem,

> Nothing rhymes
> With orange, so why
> Would anyone try?

Hmm—maybe there is a way I could sell this poem to an orange grower or drinks company or marmalade maker?

Creative writing is crucial to professional writing and you should bring all of your skills to the job at hand. It's not your magnum opus, it's not you're Eliot Prize collection, it is a good way of earning money to let you write those other things that may not pay (poets rarely earn a huge amount)—and in the meantime bringing some decent writing into the professional world. If we are seduced by Neruda's poetry, we could at least be similarly beguiled by a decent piece of copy—it takes a lot of writing to make the world go round. Surely we can make improvements as we go? Dandelions and daisies look great in the hedgerow, but isn't it nice to stumble upon a clump of bluebells or daffodils every now and then?

## What Is Professional Writing?

Let us begin by exploring what might be meant by the term *professional writing*, and particularly what it means to those of us who are writers. If we look up the word *professional* in a dictionary, the first description is that it relates to, or is characteristic of 'a profession'. Recognising writing as a profession seems like a great place to start. A profession infers members delivering to a particular standard and quality. A further description of professional is 'exhibiting a courteous, conscientious, and generally business-like manner in the workplace' (from https://www.merriam-webster.com/dictionary/professional). This too sounds applicable when considering how words are used as a major means to communication; and business-like suggests this is distinct from informal and casual forms of communication. In fact, anyone who has seen and signed a publishing contract for that novel or poetry and so on will be immediately alerted to the professionalism expected. If you are a serious writer, you will be aware that publishing is a business and the sooner you take it seriously, the better it will be for you. By all means write for pleasure, and by all means take pleasure in what you write. But if you are writing for public consumption and you want your writing to be sold and read, a standard of professionalism is a basic requirement. And like the discussion about 'creative writing' above, it is crucial that the creative and professional approach are not separated.

## Can Writing Really Be a Profession?

For those who enjoy the craft of writing, or indeed employ the craft of writing as work, it sounds ideal. But when we look at the remuneration rates for a great deal of writing work, we are also left with the important question: could anyone actually make a professional living from it? This is a question we'll explore in some depth throughout this book, because many people certainly do manage to make a living and a comfortable one. For others, however, writing is a part-time occupation, alongside other employment options that pay the bills (the struggling poet working during the day as a barista, the teacher writing her novel on weekends, the university lecturer teaching writing while writing her own book … there are plenty of examples). The fact is that for some, being a full-time writer is sadly nothing more than a nice idea and the reality of rent, food and bills stand in the way. We're not going to say it's easy and that we can help you to reverse your fortunes. But we are going to share some ideas which may help; and with sweat, perseveration and not a little knowledge about what a professional writer does, just might turn your writing into a more viable career choice.

We hope many writers (and readers hopefully) consider the art of writing to be an admirable occupation. But in using the word occupation, or even profession, comes the not unreasonable expectation that the said professional has an associated career and potential to earn a living. And it is here that many aspiring writers falter at the expectation of 'writing as a profession'. Let's face it, the reality is many experienced and budding writers need to have a 'day job' to sustain their writerly practices. This book doesn't set out to provide any golden ticket or offer a sure-fire way to suddenly amass riches through writing, because there is no such ticket. What it does aim to do is show ways in which writers can use their talents to make money. And how there are numerous options for a writer to explore, so that they can build up a multi-faceted writing career. But let us emphasise from the beginning: making a career from professional writing requires a lot of effort, perseverance, flexibility, determination and downright courage. And the best place to start is by calling yourself a 'professional writer'. If you want others to believe it, you need to believe it yourself first.

Professional writing can also be read as the opposite of 'amateur' writing, as we see here in the *Oxford English Dictionary*'s description: 'Of an event, activity, occupation, etc. (now esp. a sport): undertaken or engaged in for money; engaged in by professionals (as distinct from non-professionals or amateurs).' Being professional, or acting professionally, is an essential aspect for the 'writer as a career choice' to come to grips with. Just like the professional football player will have expectations of him/her regarding quality and performance, so too does the professional writer. If a writer wants to sell their writing services, then they have to be prepared to play with 'the best of the best'. They must be in top form and get out there and sell themselves. It's not easy and sadly, it pays nowhere near that of top football players. And I'm afraid that's where that analogy comes to an end. But what is important to remember, if you're going to charge for your writing, then those receiving your services will expect the Premier League and demand a professional service.

Let's come back to the term 'business-like', and what that then infers. We could take this very literally and assume it is for an organisation or business, and there are very clear connotations—for example, in the language and style used. It is clearly non-fiction in style (though potentially some exceptions) and while creativity is an important component, there are many differences with writing fictional work. The term 'business' can be used quite loosely—for the freelance writer, it can mean a wide variety of organisations: from limited companies, government bodies, charities, small businesses and even other freelancers. But even the creative writer operates in a professional world—they deal with agencies, publishing companies, other service providers such as editors and proof-readers. If you want to have your articles published in a magazine or online, you'll need to communicate effectively with other businesses. Many freelance writers set themselves up as independent self-employed companies, which are in effect small businesses, which have certain regulatory requirements (such as submitting business accounts). Therefore, when it comes to being professional and business-like, establishing this as a basis for getting a writing career off the ground seems like a rather solid and sensible way to go.

## This Book Approaches Professional Writing from These Three Perspectives

Firstly…

it's about *making a viable career from writing*—for example, we will explore how a writer can build up a portfolio of working options and consider how to freelance successfully. That's not to say that many of the techniques and methods discussed in the following pages apply also to writing as an employee of an organisation—but we'll be coming at it from the perspective of a writer working independently.

Secondly…

it's about *finessing the craft of writing and working at the top of the game*. Not just in the writing produced but in how a writer finds opportunities, delivers work and sells themselves. Success as a writer depends on the quality of the final product—even the most talented freelancer will fall at the final hurdle if the promised goods don't deliver to the client's expectations. Therefore, writing skills are essential.

And thirdly…

it's about *approaching writing as a career choice*. Of course, some lucky writers manage to make a living from writing novels and other fictional works. Some use their talents to write in other capacities—for example, you'll find more than a few well-respected authors writing columns for magazines and newspapers. But only a few manage to be so successful they can just sit back and write their next bestseller. For the majority of writers out there, it's about being flexible—building up a portfolio of writing gigs, forever being on the lookout for new opportunities and convincing others you're the right person for the job.

Sound like hard work? We won't lie to you; it is! Then why do it? Because, let's face it, we love to write and it's hugely rewarding when we can make a living doing something we enjoy.

# Why Is Professional Writing Critical to Business?

Take a look around and it won't take very long to find examples of poor writing and careless mistakes. This one appeared recently in a popular forest area where I like to go walking with my dog:

This didn't appear just once. Over the following weeks, numerous signs appeared throughout the area, perpetuating the same mistake. It certainly caught the attention of local walkers, alas for all the wrong reasons. Over the summer I was stopped by more than a few other walkers, some to have a chuckle, but more than a few were clearly annoyed and frustrated at yet another poor use of the English language. But this isn't just about poor writing skills; it says something about the company itself (a water provider). The sign above was place in a forest area, popular with walkers and horse riders, where a large water company was performing extensive excavation works. Okay, it's a simple error—we can all transcribe words occasionally. But this unintended mistake (and can you spot it?) reflected on the company who provided the sign and not in a good way. Not only does it show a thoughtless use of language, but a lack of checking and editing before they went ahead and had at least a dozen similar signs produced. The end result? Rather than drawing attention to the Bridle Way, it simply reflected badly on the company. I began to wonder if this rather sloppy attention to detail applied to other areas of their business. Does my water bill, for example, receive the same level of diligence?

So how do such mistakes happen? This wasn't a small business but a large nationwide utility company. Surely there must be processes in place to prevent such things. Okay, the example above isn't going to have huge detrimental effects, but there could be instances where a sign could. For example, they also dug a large hole in a road—if they got the danger sign wrong the impact of that could be life threatening.

Part of the issue comes down to time. There is the need for large volumes of communication on an ever more frequent basis, meaning that 'business writing' is often produced quickly, and needs to be delivered ever more quickly, often resulting in either rushed quality checking or not at all. Think of the number of times you have received emails that were badly written—I bet it's more than just a few. But time is not the only factor at play here and this is important. Simple, good writing skills are a 'skill' which are required by all business roles—and not everyone is skilled at writing. And to be fair, if your expertise or specialism is in a different area, you might be more focused on ensuring specific details are correct, and less aware of the art of writing, which is where you come in. You see there is a place for professional writers.

## What Are Some of the Causes of Poor Professional Writing?

- A lack of acknowledgement of writing as a crafted skill. Sometimes writing just isn't seem as that important. There are engineers, doctors, technical specialists, carpenters, plumbers and and so on, but writing isn't their job. Like them, writers have their job—and value—too.
- A lack of awareness of the intended audience. Especially if it's in a specialist area, it's very possible specialist terms will have little meaning to someone who doesn't know the field. I worked for a long time within IT departments. A great example of a department that has its own world with its own language, one that often left the rest of the business in a combination of amusement, puzzlement and bewilderment. But this is a common factor throughout the professional world.
- A lack of time and effort. We've all seen the email, statement, memo, contract (even) which has been pulled together from other pieces of writing and hatched together.

All of these are areas where the switched-on freelance writer can really make a difference. They can ask questions and ensure they know the audience; writing is their craft (that one's in the bag) and as for time and effort—put forward a winning proposal that demonstrates the small investment in a professional writer brings benefits that strongly outweigh the investment.

There is clearly a need for high-quality business writing and there is a lack of quality business writing skills within organisations. This is the gap that an astute and good professional writer can quickly fill—and indeed we have both taught students who are filling this gap (there is a lot more places to fill thought).

> **Top Tip: Hone Your Craft**
>
> To succeed as a freelance writer, you need to really perfect your craft—this means clean copy and your editing must be top notch. Just like a professional painter is expected to deliver a well-painted wall. There is no margin for error or sloppy work—your writing needs to be free of any grammatical errors and typos. Get into the habit now, of always proofreading and editing your work—or work with another writer and edit each other's!

## How Is Professional Writing Different to Other Forms of Writing?

### Lose Your Own Voice and Become an Imitator!

One of the key differences with professional writing and other forms is that you are often providing writing for someone else. You might be representing an organisation or another person, and in these situations, it is not your voice which is important. Whereas with our own creative writing, a real sense of the author comes through, an organisation often wants to have a consistent voice and image—and they should be hiring numerous writers who will all be expected to produce content in a very similar 'house' style and manner. It is not uncommon for businesses to provide a style guide, and it is good practice when delivering content for a company, say, content for their website, to review other published items. Good professional writers who regularly work with particular companies, built up a style guide that they can refer to on their next assignment. Indeed 'writing a style guide' is something you should be thinking about when engaging with a client.

## Write to Specification

Professional writing is typically about writing to a brief or specification. The writer may have very little creative license with what is produced. Sometimes the client will specify the length, what must be included, the tone, key information, as well as who it should be aimed at. The more you can get the client to specify exactly what it is they want, the easier the assignment will be. It will also reduce the possibility of the client being disappointed with what you produce, or you having to spend more time on the project because you didn't believe what they wanted.

## It May Be on a Subject You Don't Know Much About or Have Very Little Interest In

I've written articles on many subjects I knew only the basics about—but I'm a diligent researcher and can write about a wide range of topics. I used to write for a luxury wedding online magazine, producing bi-weekly content on luxury honeymoon locations, wedding preparations, bridal wear and the like. It's not something I'm even the little bit interested in, but it was relatively easy to research, and once I became familiar with the magazine style, I could very quickly adopt it.

That said, they are some subjects that I wouldn't tackle because I don't believe I'd use the right language and be able to convey an expert voice—for example, I don't know much about football (or if I am working for a US company, soccer—see, it's about getting it right).

## It's Professional

Unless the business you're writing for has a particularly funky image and is happy for you to use informal language, incautious language, slang, curse and use of profanity in its content, then it's best to err on the side of caution. Be polite, courteous and non-confrontational, if in doubt. And avoid phrases that go out of fashion very quickly. There is nothing worse than identifying with a youth audience (say) then trying to write in a way which will go out of fashion very quickly. What ever happened to groovy, cool, lush, sick (don't ask).

## The Demand for High-Quality Content and Copy

In this digital age, the demand for high-quantity content is insatiable. As consumers, we expect websites to be up to date, providing us with regular, frequent and interesting content—that is reliable. If it's not doing so, then we'll simply go elsewhere. Not only do businesses need to have product catalogues and reports, but consumers expect them to be experts in their specialism, providing frequent content that is leading edge and informative. Go to a website and discover the content hasn't been updated for a while? Then we'll go elsewhere and quickly form an opinion. Whereas in the past, businesses invested heavily in expensive marketing such as advertisements—many are now using a diverse range of marketing forums—such as social media and the rise of the 'influencer'—enabling them to utilise the budget in many varied and different ways. Think, for example, the reach of an endorsement by someone on Instagram that has a large number of followers—their readership trusts their expert opinion—and the significantly lower cost means that the business can enable a large number of such social media endorsers.

Already we're seeing that businesses need a diverse range of platforms—they might have a website, which contains articles, latest news, a blog and so on. They might also be on Twitter … and while it's an easy step to set these things up, maintaining them is something else again. The website information needs to be up to date and relevant. Blogs need to have frequent and regular posts. Twitter not only needs frequent posts, but comments need to be monitored. If you're a small business, this can all seem overwhelming—but faced with not doing it at all—could be the death of an otherwise viable business. Hiring someone full time isn't always a viable option—but a freelancing writer? That charges by the hour. They could very well be able to afford someone who could spend a few hours each week, maintaining a blog and responding to comments.

> **Top Tip: Start Small**
>
> You often don't need to look far to find a small business who would like to have a stronger social media presence. They just don't have the time or perhaps the expertise, to dedicate to the task. But they might be able to afford just a couple of hours each week, to get started. That might not seem like much work, but if you can find a handful of gigs like this—that's a day's work a week!

## Business Style and a Consistent Image

The talent of a freelance writer is to be a chameleon. In any one week I will morph into a number of different writers—one day I'm an IT writer using technical jargon, producing articles and newsletters for a company that delivers technology products. Another day I might write a proposal for a global finance company and use language that is business-like, efficient and in American English. Another week I will work for a make-up business and write blogposts on the latest trend. And on some days, I assume the role of a musician, a creative writer and so on and so forth.

What's important is that I morph myself into what the business needs:

- The first step is to *understand the business style* of the company you're writing for.
- The second step is to be able to *adopt their style*.
- The third step is to *understand the immediacy* of professional writing in a digital era.

## Key Chapter Points

- Professional writing means that you consider yourself a professional writer as much as it refers to the business clients, who you'll be providing services to.
- Mistakes in business writing are costly—to a business's bottom line and to their reputation. Get it right, and valuable business content will drive sales and help increase and retain customers.
- When we're being paid to deliver writing services, clients expect quality—just like in any other industry. So, we have to be prepared to understand what our client requires and deliver quality work.
- There's a high demand for high-quality content—we just need to get out there and find it. But that high demand means that there's a high expectation for immediacy.
- Every business/client has a 'business style'. If it's not written down, then we need to work out what it is and adopt it.

### Exercise 1.1

Don't just take our word for it …

Go online and see how quickly you can find a website with:

- Content that hasn't been updated in the past six months or more
- Out-of-date content
- Webpages with typos or grammatical errors
- Web content with incorrect facts

You've found your first potential customer!

## Exercise 1.2

Let's get some practice….

You've been contracted to write a number of blog posts for a content providing agency.

The clients include:

- A language school promoting learning retreats
- A children's party organiser
- An IT provider specializing in networking products
- A company that manufactures surf boards
- A self-employed yoga instructor
- A local charity that provides meals for the homeless
- A nursery specialising in exotic plants

Consider for each:

- Word choice—what style and tone—might be appropriate?
- What image might they be trying to portray?
- Who might be their target audience?

# 2

## Writing for Business

In this chapter we will:

1. Explore the different types of writing that are found in businesses, both internally (that's the communications that occur inside the company) and externally (and that's to external sources).
2. Consider the language and tone that we might use for different clients and situations.
3. Discuss how to up our game and behave like professional writers.

> \* Deut. 5.
> 16.mat.
> 15.4.
> ephe 6.2.
> \* Matth.
> 5.23.
>
> 12 ¶ * Honour thy father and thy mother, that thy dayes may bee long vpon the land which the LORD thy God giueth thee.
> 13 * Thou shalt not kill.
> 14 Thou shalt commit adultery.
> 15 Thou shalt not steale.
> 16 Thou shalt not beare false witnesse against thy neighbour.
>
> \* Rom.
> 7.7.
>
> 17 * Thou shalt not couet thy nighbours house, thou shalt not couet thy neighbours wife, nor his man-seruant, nor his maid-seruant, nor his oxe, nor

In 1631, Robert Barker and Martin Lucas, the Royal printers, lost their publishing licence and were fined £300 after the typo in this (can you spot it?). That's around £38,000 (or 53,000 USD) in today's money. A big price to pay for missing out three small letters in a version of the Bible. In late May 2017, the White House released a statement saying one of President Donald Trump's goals during his trip to Israel was to "promote the possibility of lasting peach" in the region. And these are just two examples which demonstrate how the written word and communication can have huge implications for a business or organisation. And it's not only small businesses that make mistakes!

There is no avoiding the simple fact; companies need to communicate and communicating well and properly is important. Actually, it's not just important, it's essential! Whether it's amongst its employees, with customers, attracting potential clients, negotiating with external providers, liaising with government institutions … the list goes on. Communication is serious business for any organisation and can make all the difference between success and failure.

From an external perspective, communication is how a business will convince a marketplace that they need their products, skills and/or services. A company needs to 'talk' to their customers, build relationships, establish needs and wants, as well as responding to enquires and requests. Employees need to discuss long and short-term plans, agree product strategies, identify target markets, discuss financial budgets, design proposals, write reports. And it's not just what you say, it's how you say it.

Through words and pictures a business portrays an image, which in turn attracts customers. Think about the different shops you'll see along a high street or in a shopping centre. The sign above the door says as much about the business as the displays in the window. What the name is, the font used, the size, the colour … and that's before we've even gone through the door. Get it wrong and they'll fail to attract the customers they need to make profit. Now of course, this is the work of marketers and imagineers, but carrying this message through every communication that represents the company identity is crucial.

Internally businesses have an immense need to convey messages, evaluate masses of data, assess choices and make decisions. In a rapidly changing environment, the method and format of communication is constantly evolving, but what remains a constant is the need for clear, reliable and suitable communication. We have all experienced the badly written email and the repercussions of poor communication. See the examples below: this is poor communicating. While it might seem ridiculous that such a situation could occur in the first place, but for the disabled person who wants to park their car, this is a very serious issue:

In the sign below, someone's attempt at clever use of design and language has really missed the mark and resulted in a confusing message:

These pencils were sent out to an elementary school in New York in 1998. They were recalled after a student pointed out the embarrassing message that appeared after sharpening a pencil. But sadly, for the company involved, the mistake was avoidable—and a quick Google search will reveal this mistake isn't going away:

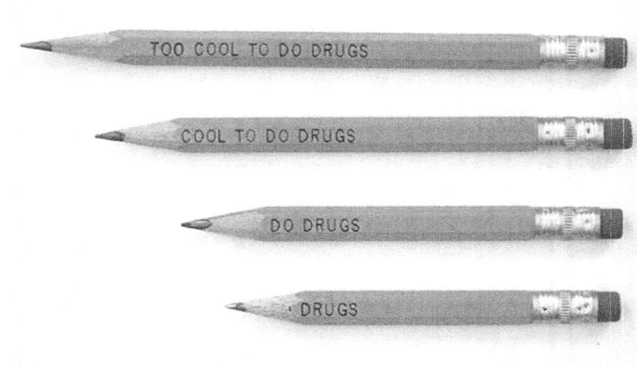

## External Communication

It wasn't so long ago that businesses would communicate with their customers via handwritten letters. But with the arrival of mass marketing in the form of electronic media, the demand for content has increased exponentially. The rise of the advertisements and associated brands and images, through media forms such as newspapers, television, expanded into the electronic media we have today; all of it bombarding the potential buyer with words and images. And of course, with social media now playing a strong role, if anything, communication is only becoming more and more frequent. However, while it continues to play an ever-dominant role, it has evolved and continues to morph according to the needs and demands of the marketplace. Meanwhile, the consumer has become more savvy and wary of advertising. The way we consume information has changed. Many of us are less inclined to read lengthy newspapers and tend to acquire informational diets in smaller bite-sized chunks on a lot more frequent basis—snacking regularly rather than three square meals a day—Twitter and Instagram being the perfect examples.

For the freelance writer this opens up a lot of potential. Businesses of all shapes and sizes are confronted with this demand for constant content—for their marketing material, for their social media sites, for their blogs—and they don't always have the staff or skills to deliver it. This is where you can come in. We have come across many students in our classes who have gone on to make jobs for themselves, sometimes by telling employers (diplomatically, of course) what they don't realise they need—but need it they very much do.

# Internal Communication

While external communication is often directly correlated to revenue generation, internal communication can sometimes be considered the 'poor' cousin often attracting much less attention at getting it right. But internal means of exchanging information can be costly if not done well.

Emails, meeting minutes, office memos are basic forms of office communication that typically all employees are expected to produce and are churned out in hundreds if not thousands, daily across all companies. While it is internal and means that there is less risk of causing significant risk to company reputation if it goes wrong, there is still potential to cause upset, trouble, confusion, and can waste time and impact on productivity. Poor communication leads to lost time, bad hiring, failed recruitment, extended time to market, lost sales and opportunities, missed innovation, poorly functioning teams, low motivation and, of course, wasted resources.

The cost of poor communication in any organisation is high, as can be seen in these two surveys:

- The top three reasons why people do not like their jobs are communication related: lack of direction from management, poor communication overall and constant change that is not well communicated. (2014 survey from About.com)
- A survey of 400 companies with 100,000 employees each cited an average loss per company of USD 62.4 million per year because of inadequate communication to and between employees. (David Grossman, "The Cost of Poor Communications," The Holmes Report, 17 July 2011)

With the rise of global companies and offices located all over the world to people working from home in an electronic age—whether we like it or not, emails and messages/texts has become a major form of communication.

Then there are other, much more significant documents that are the foundation for decisions: reports, proposals, terms of reference. What's key with all these forms of writing is that the content needs to convey the message succinctly, clearly and with no ambiguity as to its intended outcome. You would be surprised how difficult this is.

Many freelancers find work filling such communication gaps in for businesses. We can't speak for Donald Trump and his tweeting, but even top sports people such as players in the NBA or Premier League footballers have people tweeting on their behalf—so they can avoid the inevitable pitfalls and *faux pas*. But even important tasks such as writing reports and proposals, especially for a small business, can become problematic if there just isn't the staff or the skills internally. Having freelance writing skills, you can provide this as a service and can address this issue for them—and if it's a writer the company have worked with previously, who understands their communication and writing style, or who can work with them, even better.

> **Top Tip: What's the Objective?**
>
> To avoid ambiguity always understand your client's objective before you start a writing gig. Sometimes, in their enthusiasm, they tell you *what* they want, not *why* they want it. For example, if they're looking to target a different audience than their product usually attracts, you might approach you're writing differently. And don't forget their *business style*—what you might find exceedingly funny might be interpreted differently and cost you dearly.

# Business Language and Tone

## How We Communicate Creates an Image

The name of a business, the words and tone of its advertising, the language it uses in its communication with its customers, the subjects it blogs about—these are just a few ways that words form the image of a business. Get it wrong and you send out the wrong signals. For example, its old news now but as we were writing this, a Christmas advert from exercise bike company Peloton was widely mocked on social media as being "sexist", "out of touch" and even "dystopian" (https://www.bbc.co.uk/news/business-50649826; accessed 30 January 2020) and subsequently it was reported that the company lost approximately USD 1.6 billion in their market value (https://www.cbsnews.com/news/peloton-bike-ad-even-wall-street-hates-the-controversial-peloton-bike-ad-today-2019-12-05/; accessed 2 January 2020). That was communication at its worst. Get it right and you reinforce a brand, an image, a message. Get it wrong and it can backfire spectacularly. And with the speed a message can spread online, the damage can be impossible to contain. Where in the past you could remove a billboard that contained a mistake, today in our digital world, errors or even misinterpretations can be broadcast swiftly and once it goes viral there's no stopping or recalling it because it crosses platforms (Facebook/Instagram/Twitter/TV) very quickly.

It's unlikely you will be invited onto a major, international advertising campaign when you're just starting out, however any communication, regardless of the size of the company, can have an impact. For example, a company's website does much more than simply tell us what they do. It portrays the corporate image, telling us something about what the company is like (fun-lovely, ethical, technological, as just a few examples). But whether is a small startup company or a major international brand (which was a startup once), the way it presents itself is very important. So too the way it follows through and behaves on sites such as Twitter, as part of its communication package. Think of those businesses that particularly attract you? Is it something about how they engage with you that forms part of the connection? Even something as simple as responding on social media creates an impression—and while small businesses may not have the staff available to monitor their sites, engaging a freelancer to spend a few hours a day to reply to comments, but just be worth the investment. A major US bank decided it wanted to encourage its audience to save money by tweeting about their customers bad spending habits. As you can probably imagine, not everyone saw the funny side. In April this year, a small online company that I follow on Instagram ran a post declaring that they were changing their product range to now specialise exclusively in expensive t-shirts. I was rather unimpressed and after a long day working had completely forgotten it was April Fool's Day. I didn't realise until a month later that it was actually a prank. I wonder how many customers, just like me, had unfollowed them thinking they were no longer relevant to them.

With all this in mind, the first step in being an effective freelance writer is to get to grips with the business' image and style. Let's have a look at a few brands, not because we want to promote them, but to consider the image they want to portray to their potential market.

Crumpler is an Australian company selling bags—backpacks, messenger bags and so on. This is how they describe themselves:

> From Melbourne's laneways to the world's highways and airways, Crumpler is driven by new ideas, and doing things better, in our own unique way. (https://www.crumpler.com/au/; accessed 13 December 2019)

Here's a description for one of their bags:

> Crumpler's Waxed Canvas bags will age with class and distinction like a fine wine. Soft to the touch, they will maintain the weatherproofing and durability of a Traditional Waxed Canvas. Our Canvas is crafted to develop a unique character over time that reflects your adventures together.
>
> **Jumbuck**:   Name your adventure and the Jumbuck pouch is ready. Bustling market, street party, casual city ramble: attach the shoulder strap, pack your essentials and leave the baggage at base camp. (https://www.crumpler.com/au/; accessed 13 December 2019)

Already, from their brief description we discover something of how this business formed. That it is from Melbourne's 'laneways' (for example) suggests it was once a small startup in what sounds like a rather creative, funky district. And how do they want the reader to think of them? A funky, friendly company, bringing new ideas, doing things better, in a unique way.

Now let's consider the bag description: *Age with class and distinction like a fine wine.* This hints strongly at the consumer they'd like to attract—one that also enjoys fine wine and has the money to buy it. And for the customer of their Jumbuck bag—they're an adventurous soul who'll be found in a bustling market or street party. Are they aiming for the retired traveller? Unlikely. They are looking at a younger, upwardly mobile demographic. Already from these few lines, we get a feel for their target customer.

In contrast, let's look at the high-end car brand, Jaguar (https://www.jaguar.co.uk).

Not surprisingly we see terms such as pulse-quickening sports cars, but not far down their website page is their lifestyle collections, which is described as:

> Pack a little style for your journey with our collection of apparel and gifts. Choose from driving jackets, perfect polos and branded shades, and a range of luggage to carry it all in.

Whereas Crumpler is using language which will appeal to the younger, more rugged (rumpled—which crumple suggests) travelling adventurer, here the tone is different. It's more luxurious and tapping into a market where money is of little object, with driving jackets, branded shades and so on.

## Identifying the Subject, Audience and Objective

Whether it's a text, an email or any form of communication, getting it right comes down to three things:

1. Know the subject.
2. Know the audience.
3. Understand the objective.

Whether the subject is a backpack or a test-driving a luxury car, we need to be clear what it is we are promoting with the writing. One of Crumpler's bags is called 'Veggie Leather'. Do they know their target consumer? They sure do.

While it's a bag like many of their others, the distinguishing feature of this one is the material it's made out of.

Who is the audience Jaguar are aiming to reach? Given a lot of their cars start at £60,000 it's fair to say their target market are not looking for budget cars. So rather than using terms like bustling or rambling, they are using more refined language—such as breath-taking luxury saloon.

Such as with the Jaguar text—the pulse-quickening sports car line was used when trying to attract readers to take a test drive, whereas the description to promote one of their saloon cars is: breath-taking luxury saloon, spacious and beautiful yet powerfully agile.

## Reader-Friendly Writing and Readability

Ensuring the writing, hits the mark, when it comes to the target audience, is key. Once the objective is clear—whether that is getting the potential client to book a test drive, enticing them to buy a backpack, convince them of the virtues of eating cupcakes—it's about conveying the message in a way that works for the intended audience. Identify that target audience and the freelancer has a good chance of writing content that will deliver its intention.

## Sentence Structure and Word Choice

And then it comes down to basics. Any content has to appear as though it's been written and produced by the business's communication 'team'—even if that team doesn't even exist. Look at *Crumpler* example—they've carefully selected words that will appeal to their target audience. They'll know what a city ramble is and feel comfortable putting their laptop in a messenger bag. Even their name is a careful derivative—the word *Crumpler* comes from its first bearer, who was a person with an abnormal curvature of the spine. The surname *Crumpler* is derived from the Old English word 'crump', which *means* bent or crooked. So, we can take it this isn't the image they are conveying. It's more likely trying to convey a look, a rumpled, crumpled, scrunched, uncompromising, functional, bendable, understated, urban expedition, quick turnaround, all-purpose, no-fuss idea.

And if you read their website, you will see their sentences are short and snappy; they don't waste words or expect their reader want to read a load of text. They load the words onto the image they are trying to present.

> **Top Tip: If Using Images Make Sure You Have Permission**
>
> If you're providing images with your text, you have a few options. You can take photographs yourself, which avoids any copyright issues. But if this isn't an option, then you need to do some searching. If using an image found online, you must have copyright permission to use it, unless it explicitly states that it is 'free for commercial use and no attribution required'.

# Engaging with Readers

## The Way of Communication

New media dictates communication is becoming ever fast paced, more frequent and personalised. Long letters are few and far between and we almost know what the former president of the United States is thinking before he does with his immediate and frequent tweets. More often today, businesses will communication with their clients via short emails or social media comments. Messages are conveyed in different methods and formats, aiming at more than just attracting interest. It's about engagement. It's about establishing a bond between audience and brand. They'd love nothing more than to form a long-lasting relationship with us.

## Pressure to Stay in Touch

And it's not just the ways and formats that have changed; it's also the frequency. Companies are under immense pressure to stay in contact—whether that be in regular blog posts, updated articles on online media—if they want to appear as experts in their fields. While the methods of communication have increased exponentially and seemingly with very little investment (the cost for a small business to invest in a website, e.g., can be very minimal), there is the resultant demand for constant content that is stimulating, relevant, accurate and appealing to the potential market.

## It's All About Image

A company's 'image' is all important. It makes a brand recognisable in a consumer's eyes and will hugely influence whether that consumer will become a customer—and not just a one-off purchaser, but a loyal customer who will return for future purchases.

Regardless of what that image is, a business needs to convey itself as professional. They might be hip, funky and fun-lovely, but they are still professional and value their customers highly. To ensure this image is portrayed at all times, behind the scenes there are processes and mechanisms in place to ensure that's exactly the image the consumer gets to see at all time.

Which is where the writer comes to the fore—its words that are driving this communication. *What* and *how* the message is communicated has a huge impact on what is received—not to mention the detrimental impact poor communication can have. Incorrect facts, mistakes and grammatical errors, reflect on a business. This cannot be over-emphasised.

## Writing Professionally and the Freelancer

And if you're the business—and as a freelancer, that's very much the case—having strong writing skills is essential. And if the freelancer is trying to establish themselves, the more aspects of running a business they can do themselves, the more they can limit their expenses. Whether it's writing a business case to secure funding, writing proposals to win work, or maintaining communication with customers—professional writing skills are an essential component to freelancing. But if you are freelancing as a writer, your communication takes on another perspective. It's showcasing your writing abilities while touting for the work those abilities deserve. How much work do your efforts deserve? It's a question we should all ask ourselves.

> **Top Tip: Always Check If Your Client Uses British or American English**
> If they don't have a style guide, The Writers online resource is a good start for the basics: http://www.thewriter.com

## The Professional Freelancer …

…*understands exactly what's required*. Focus on the five big questions:

- Who is it for? The audience.
- What is it? The product.
- When is it needed by? The deadline.
- Where is it for? The medium.
- Why is it needed? The objective.

If these questions aren't answered in the brief, then have a call or email with the client will help to get them clarified and avoids costly re-work if you've got it wrong.

*…is organised.* Your chaotic student days are over. No more working late nights and hoping you can wing it with an all-night writing session. Clients just aren't going to pay for that type of behaviour. That want to see that your well organised and approach your writing in a structured manner. They might not see that messy desk or post-it notes all over the floor, but a lack of organisation can show in your writing.

*…is a professional.* They agree any work, no matter how small, with an agreement. This doesn't need to be long—a brief one-page word document is fine; in some instances it can also be an email. But a professional freelancer doesn't start work until they have the agreed with their client. And once the job is finished, they send an invoice. Small things do make a difference—such as having a professional email address and details at the bottom of every email. Act professionally and your clients will soon treat your professionally.

*…works to a to-do list.* We find that a three-list approach works well:

1. The three things you must do today.
2. The three things that you'd like to get done today.
3. The three things you need to get done sometime soon.

## Key Chapter Points

1. Mistakes do happen and are not only costly to a business, they also affect a writer's reputation. That client may not commission you again for work, and if it's published online, it might be a legacy you (and they) wish would go away.
2. Understand the company's image before you start writing for them. Ensure your words and copy reflect the type of business they are and the impression they want to make.
3. Always engage with your client and understand their objective with the project they are wanting you to undertake.
4. Before you put pen to paper (or your fingers to the keyboard): know your subject, know your audience and understand the objective.
5. As a freelance writer, everything you do is a representation of your professional skills—a lack of organisation skills will reflect in many things—from poorly drafted emails to missed appointments to misunderstandings over the brief. It's important to convey a professional image at all times.

## Exercise 2.1 Know Your Client!

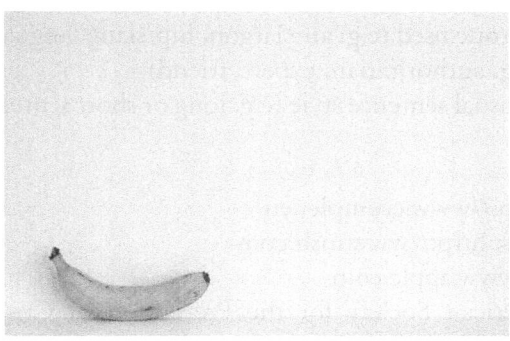

You've been commissioned to write an article about bananas. How might it differ depending on the client?

1. The International Banana Association: http://www.banana.org
2. Local supermarket
3. Local doctor's surgery
4. The World Banana Forum: http://www.fao.org/world-banana-forum/en/
5. Online cake and recipe website
6. A local primary school
7. The Australian Banana Growers: https://abgc.org.au
8. The World Health Organisation
9. Local café
10. Dentist website
11. Website for pregnant women
12. Weight loss website
13. Skin care website
14. Haircare website
15. Banana Republic: https://www.bananarepublic.co.uk

## Exercise 2.2 Identify the Client's Writing Style
You have won a bid to write a website article for each of the companies below. Before writing the article, review their existing website and identify the writing style for each:
  Describe:

1. The image they are portraying (e.g. formal, casual, serious, fun, technological, informative)
2. The language/tone used (e.g. any jargon, hip/slang language, expert terms)
3. Their style (e.g. authoritarian, expert, friend)
4. What is their usual sentence style (e.g. long or short sentences, professional or casual)?

Crumpler: http://www.crumpler.eu
Lush cosmetics: http://www.lush.com
Apple: http://www.apple.com
ASPCA—American Society for the Prevention of Cruelty to Animals: http://www.aspca.org
Planet Ark: https://planetark.org/

# 3

# A Career in Professional Writing

In this chapter we will:

- Look at how we can turn our writing into a paying proposition—that's right, making a career out of it!
- Explore the different types of roles a writer can find in business.
- Cover the various things you need to do, to go from someone who writes to someone who writes professionally.
- Reflect on the life of a freelancer (and I'm afraid it's not all guitar playing/surfing in the morning, and a few hours writing in the afternoon … well, not for all of us!).

## Writing as a Profession in Business

When considering writing as a career, flexibility is key. It doesn't take more than a quick check to know poets don't make huge amounts of income. This doesn't mean you cannot use your poetry skillset, but in financial terms the situation is worse than it looks. In a survey taken with 50,000 authors, CREATe Centre (www.create.ac.uk), School of Law, University of Glasgow, reported that the 'median' earnings of 'primary occupation authors' in 2018 was £10,497 (https://www.create.ac.uk/blog/2019/05/02/uk-authors-earnings-and-contracts-2018-a-survey-of-50000-writers/; accessed 14 January 2020). Thus, you will see even famous writers taking commissions to write for magazines, journals and so on:

**From the ecstatic comedy of Portnoy's Complaint to the narrative richness of his American Trilogy, Philip Roth was a writer of genuine originality, says Martin Amis**
   Portnoy's Complaint (1969) was my introduction to Philip Roth. I read it in the first edition of the paperback, and I thought: here we have a really deafening new voice, and a whole new way of being funny—transgressive, corrosive, but with something ecstatic in its comedy. (https://www.theguardian.com/books/2018/may/26/martin-amis-on-philip-roth-the-kind-of-satirical-genius-that-comes-along-once-in-a-generation; accessed 14 January 2020)

It's great that Martin Amis can gives us his views on Phillip Roth, but it would be naïve to think he published this for free. There was another widely read *Guardian* newspaper article that said,

The arts world was divided between shock and hilarity last night at the news that the latest novel from the best-selling author Fay Weldon has been sponsored by the Italian jewelry firm Bulgari—with a requirement in her contract for at least a dozen mentions of its products. (https://www.theguardian.com/uk/2001/sep/04/pressandpublishing.fiction; accessed 14 January 2020)

Not all of us are going to get such high-profile commissions, but we all have to earn a living somehow. Therefore, the more skills a professional writer can bring to the role of being a writer, the more they can potentially offer as a means of earning while writing their magnum opus (if that is your wish). If you are going to be a professional writer, you have to think like one by considering the options you have to even make a living income.

Some skills complement each other nicely, such as copywriting and editing. Writing your novel in the morning, editing someone else's copy in the afternoon. But whatever the paid work, when freelancing, there are two aspects to consider:

- A potential client generally wants someone who can complete work effectively and efficiently—that doesn't mean that you need to be an 'expert' in the subject, but that you know enough to be competent. If it's a detailed piece on a particular topic, then you may very well need to be an expert; if it's a basic introductory piece, then being able to research well, may be the skills required. What's key is to be able to convince the potential client that you have the required skills and that you're the person for the work. If they need the piece within a deadline, having someone who can deliver a quality piece in the required timeframe is key.

- A freelancer needs to have many strings to their bow—and to different clients you'll appear differently. And that's fine. Therefore, creating a few personas will help you transition between different pieces of work. It's now well known that Salman Rushdie came up with 'irresistibubble' for Aero and 'Naughty but Nice' for cream cakes when he worked in advertising, but there will have been many he is less proud of.

But let's begin with some basics of writing jobs. If you freelancing as a writer, it's very likely you'll work in a number of these roles, perhaps even at the same time.

## Jobs Available to Professional Writers

Writing is at the heart of many roles we see in businesses. There are very few jobs today that don't involve communicating, and therefore, writing, to some extent. However, while word processors and software might have done away with the typewriter, a skilled and talented wordsmith is still a sought-after and valued commodity, as the following roles demonstrate:

**Advertising Copywriters.** Many writers utilise their writing skills and abilities to persuade, to create captivating copy for print, television, radio and online advertising. A good advertising copywriter can make an audience want a particular product or service. This can include creative content such as slogans, billboards, radio jingles, or social media ads. You'll be able to say a lot with just a few words. While landing a job in an advertising agency can be tough (there's a lot of competition), all businesses need advertising—this includes sole traders, small local businesses and charities. Start small and build up your experience.

**Bloggers.** There are many independent bloggers out there, so trying to get yours to standout is a tough call—let alone trying to earn any money from blogging. But bloggers themselves can write for third parties. Loads of businesses how have blogs connected with their websites—it's a great way for them to demonstrate they are industry experts—but they need quality content. This is where the talented blogger can step in. You won't make a fortune, but it's experience and if you can land a few of these gigs, it can provide an income.

**Book Editors.** These suggest changes and improvements to an author's manuscript and are responsible for getting it ready for publication. They're able to bring a fresh eye to the manuscript and work with the author to strengthen the fundamentals and structure of the story. Many editors work for publishing houses, but other editors go freelance and offer the same services to writers seeking help. With more and more writers finding it increasingly difficult to get the traditional agents to notice their work, having a talented book editor improve your work has become ever more popular.

**Communications Specialists.** Many organisations, especially the larger ones, will have communications departments with a range of roles. This can include positions such as the Communications Director—something to work towards—but there are also positions, such as Website Manager and Public Relations Manager, who deliver a consistent voice for the business. Communications officers create content that furthers an organisation's marketing goals. This can include material such as brochures, e-books, press releases and so on. This role involves making sure that all written content follows branding guidelines and uses the company's voice and image. Knowledge of the particular industry the company is in is also essential, along with strong persuasive writing expertise.

**Content Marketing Specialists.** Publishing great content—whether articles, video or infographics—is an increasingly popular way for brands to attract and increase their audience. All of these forms need great copy, so goods writers who can write great marketing content are sought after.

**Copywriters.** These (like Salman Rushdie mentioned above) produce *copy* for businesses. It's often associated with adverting and promotional material, but actually copy can mean many things. Sometimes it can just be about informing. Copywriters typically provide the text, or 'copy', which appears on brochures, posters, websites, emails, advertisements, catalogues and so on. It can be in print or more often than not, it's online. Some copywriters choose to specialise, becoming experts in a particular field or subject/s. But there are also businesses who need people that can produce quality copy from the content they provide—meaning copywriters can become experts in providing high-quality copy regardless of the subject matter. Having research skills is good and demonstrates, even if it's not your area of expertise, that you're happy to find out what you need to know to produce quality copy.

**Critics.** A critic writes a review—it might be for a book, a TV show, a movie, a play, a restaurant and so on—basically anything that people are interested in. Some bloggers select a niche and build up a following by offers reviews—I know of one creative writing student who wrote reviews of local plays and performances. Before long she had enough followers to allow her to approach theatres and they would give her a ticket for free; in return she would write a review. Nowadays, she has even more followers and big theatres also send her tickets. She's not being paid in money, but the way she looks at it, she's writing about something she enjoys—so it's not really hard work—and she does not have to buy show tickets. But being a good critic involves more than just getting to watch something/attending something for free. Your critique needs to be an informative review that draws people in. Just saying you love or hate it, isn't going to cut it with today's tough audiences. You'll need to make your piece stand out, and you'll need additional information (such as some knowledge about the cast or production, for example).

**Editors.** There are many publications out there that seek content from contributions. It's the editor's job to select those most appropriate to include, and to ensure they are written to the required standard. That's the role of an editor. Finding a small publication can be a great way to get started. It might be, for example, a small charity publication. It can give you the opportunity to demonstrate your talents and you just don't know who might see your work. It's also helps when you want to go for other editorial roles, to have experience on your CV.

**Email Marketeers.** Email marketing is direct marketing, uses emails to communication messages to an audience. This might be for commercial or informative reasons, and the aim of the email is to get a potential or current customer to take some sort of action. It might seem outdated with new automated developments, and with all of us receiving so many emails daily, many will go straight into trash without being read. But it's still a big industry requiring good writers. An interest in design will help, as well as a willingness to learn HTML and CSS.

**Ghost Writers.** If you don't mind seeing you work with someone else's name against it, then this might be an option. You're basically an anonymous writer and your client owns it—meaning they can claim credit for it. Might not sound like a great proposition, but many writers do make a living for helping others write their story.

**Grant Writers.** These produce proposals to secure financial support for foundations, non-profit agencies and other organisations. Grants are key method of raising funds, and while grant writers identify funding sources, they also develop written materials that target potential donors. It is a skillset which is much in demand.

**Greeting Card Writers.** You'll need to be able to write concise verses that trigger people's emotions—whether it's a humorous birthday greeting, a sentimental anniversary message, or a heartfelt get-well-soon card, the art is to come up with something that many people can relate to. Playing around with rhymes, allusions and metaphors can be good practice.

**Journalists.** These usually work in news and magazine publishing, but there can be crossover. It can be exciting and fast-paced work, but competition is high, and postgraduate degrees are dedicated to the craft. However, this shouldn't deter anyone from trying to find work and much smaller publications are always in need of contributors. Especially if you have an 'angle'—someone not far from the writer of these words wrote for parenting and maternity magazines (at a particular time in her life). Also, it would be fair to say that 'experts' come from many directions. It's not so long ago that ecological ideas, veganism and climate change were considered minority views and the environmental activist Greta Thunberg is a voice without being the world's greatest expert.

**Proposal Writers.** These prepare documents related to pricing, marketing and product design. They assess requests for proposals (RFPs) and develop responses to help individuals and businesses win new business and secure contracts. All freelance writers are in effect proposal writers and they need to outline what it is they will deliver and for what price. To do this job well you need excellent organisational and writing skills as well as an eye for detail.

**Proof-readers.** Copy needs to be checked for errors before getting published. Proof-readers check documents for all types of mistakes—simple and complex. This includes spelling mistakes and grammar errors, and the job is not complete until the document is completely error-free. Having an eye for detail is essential, as is a drive for perfection to spot inaccuracies.

**Public Relations Experts.** Analyse a business to find the positive messages and translate these into positive media stories. Copy is needed for press releases, publicity material and client promotions. While larger organisations will have public relation departments, in small businesses, it's often the owner who tries to cover this role (meaning it can get neglected).

**SEO (Search Engine Optimisation) Experts.** SEO is a fast-growing market, and an understanding of the written word can be extremely useful. An SEO expert looks at content and identifies improvements for both search engines and readers. They also produce content to publicise clients and projects. An interest in web design, programming and marketing helps, and you'll need solid technical knowledge to back you up.

**Speech Writers.** It's not just politicians and government officials that need speeches—business executives and anyone (including Uncle Joe at your cousin's wedding) can often need the services of a professional writer. To do this job effectively, you need to be able to write persuasively. Toastmasters or observing debates is a good starting place.

**Social Media Specialists.** These specialists manage social media marketing campaigns and day-to-day activities including maintaining posts and responding to comments. They develop relevant content topics to reach the target audients. They also produce, curate and manage all published content including images, video and written material. Knowing what to write to engage an audience is key. It's not always the most technically precise field—language and grammar can sometimes undergo some pretty drastic editing when faced by tight character limits. Be prepared to dive deep into statistics and metrics, as the role is as much about proving what you say is effective as it is the content itself.

**Technical Writers.** These writers have the ability to take complex technical ideas and jargon and turn it into plain English which the average reader can understand. These writers design and develop things like software manuals, user guides, FAQs, technical specifications, supporting material and other complex documentation. You need to have good technical knowledge of the area (e.g. IT, but it could just as well be engineering or manufacturing). And you'll need to be able to work with software developers, engineers and other professionals, so good interpersonal skills are essential. And let's be honest, anyone who has worked with IT manuals and so on knows there really is a huge need for clarity to cut through the fog of jargon and technicality.

**Translator.** If you're fluently in more than one language, then translation services are a good way to utilise your writing skills. You need meticulous attention to detail, and this isn't about changing or making improvements to the text—you have to translate it exactly how it is.

**Travel Writers.** If you enjoy seeing the world and being on the move, then what better way to make a living. But you need to be flexible as this is a very popular market (understandably). You need to be knowledgeable (and that means that you've been there and experienced the place) and can write guidebooks, magazine features, blogs and how-to-travel pieces in new and interesting ways.

**Video Game Writers.** Many games have elaborate narratives behind them, with players constantly making decisions that determine how the story develops and what happens to the characters. In this role, you'll develop characters, and write scenes and dialog to fit different possibilities.

**Web Content Writers.** Many businesses need writers who are highly skilled in researching and writing digital content like blogs, articles and website pages. You might need to be competent at conducting online and interviewing subject matter experts to gather information. Having knowledge of search engine optimisation (SEO) techniques is essential, and it helps to be familiar with HTML and CSS.

**Web Content Editors.** Many businesses needing dedicated web content editors to ensure the quality of their online material. Interest in the subject/field helps, as is a willingness to understand reader statistics and the role of content in search engine algorithms.

Wow! That's a lot of roles and we were only just getting started. You'll very likely be able to find others out there. You might be thinking, these all sound great, but I'm lacking experience. How do you go from being, say, a creative writing student, poet, novelist to a paid writer?

Have a look through the list and see which ones you find the most appealing. This will help you focus your skills and where to start building up your experience. I've come across many students who were surprised to discover that their extensive experience in playing video games might actually contribute to finding a proper job—but you need to bear in mind that jobs such as video game writer are highly sought after. Therefore, by all means have your goals, but be realistic. You might need to spend some years gaining experience before you can land your dream job. And if you want to make a living from freelancing, it will probably mean you'll need to be able to move between a number of these roles.

## Turning Your Written Words into a Paying Proposition

If you want someone to pay for your writing, then the first step is to

- identify how you can make a valuable contribution and
- then convince them that your writing is worth paying for because you are a professional writer.

From the very beginning, call *yourself a professional writer*. This is important. Don't allude to being a poet earning a bit on the side, or a novelist taking a paying job to get by. If you don't think of yourself as a professional writer than you're going to have a tough job trying to convince someone else. Hold your head high and repeat after me: I am a professional writer. Say it every morning in the mirror until eventually one morning you'll say, okay I get it, this is what I do for a living. When people ask what you do, you reply, 'I'm a professional writer.'

**Create a professional presence online**. This means:

- Setup a dedicated email address for your freelance writing work. It's never a good idea to use your personal email address for work.
- Create a website for your freelance writing. If you have a website already for blogging or say your creative writing—that's great. But setup another website, separate from your personal ones, for your freelance writing. It doesn't have to be fancy or cost a lost—website platforms such as Wix,

Blogger and Tumblr, all provide free templates that you can quickly tailor to your needs. This is one Lisa prepared for Andrew earlier: https://andymelrose99.wixsite.com/mysite.

- Have an active presence online—this means having a social media profile. That doesn't mean you should be spending hours every day online, browsing and catching up on tweets. But you should have a social media strategy that is manageable. It might mean having an Instagram account so that you can follow potential customers, have a schedule for posting and a way for potential customers to contact you. And with Instagram, by all means have your holiday snaps account but have one solely for business. Separate your personal and business accounts.
- LinkedIn—this gets a special mention as it's your online resume. Keep it up to date. Everything you get a writing gig, add it on here and don't forget to try and get a testimonial from the client. It's also a way for future clients to find you, to build up your network of other freelance writers and to find work (there is a job board).

**Announce to the world you're a professional writer.** (Okay, maybe not the world, but at least announce it to your family, friends and any work colleagues). You might be surprised who is in need of some professional writing. It's possible there are business owners, of all shapes and sizes, amongst your family and friends. And it's very feasible some of them might be in need of some help—especially if they own a very small business or startup. The work could be as small as editing their resume or writing an ad to drum up business. While these might be very small pieces of work, they give you writing samples that can go into your portfolio. And there's no reason why family and friends can't also provide you with some testimonials provided you have done work for them.

**Get some business cards produced.** It's also important to be ready at all times for potential writing gigs in your day-to-day life. This means creating business cards that you can quickly give to friends and family. It's great to tell people you're a writer and available for work, but they need a way to remember you and get in contact. A memorable business card means they won't forget you, and of course, sending them your online social media details is a good idea. (Go online to sites such as Canva—they have professional looking templates, and you can print off cards easily and have them delivered to your door.)

**A professional headshot.** You won't always need this, but it's handy to have one ready, just in case you do—and it's an online visual world, so it's very likely it will come in handy. Make sure, when you're asked for a photo, provide one that looks professional. A well-done headshot portrays confidence, competence, and conveys to potential clients that you are serious about what you do. It's a very important part of your branding as a freelancer. It's probably best not to use a selfie or crop yourself out of that family shot around the Christmas table. If your budget can stretch to an actual photographer, great, otherwise ask around—there's potentially a budding photographer who can help you out (and you can give them a testimonial). Some tips for the photo: keep it professional—so unless you're a skydiving instructor, that great shot of you jumping out of a plane isn't going to cut it. It's a headshot—so that means hair neat and tidy, so that your face can be seen, no sunglasses (ordinary glasses are fine) and a smile. That last point is important—it shows you are friendly and approachable.

**Your author bio.** Having a few author bios ready to go (with some minor updates) can save you time when you're rushing to submit your work. So, when you have a few spare minutes, drafting your author bio is time well spent. Having a few on hand, tailored for specific skills or industries, is a good idea. For example, I have one for IT work and a very different one for my blogging.

Tips for writing your author bio:

- Check any guidelines for the site you are submitting to and conform to them.
- Write in the third person. It comes across as having been written by an objective party.
- Stick to the facts—potential clients will search you online, so be sure that nothing you say can be proven incorrect.
- List relevant education and experience—not your life history.
- Include memberships if relevant (and these must be relevant but can also be tailored, a membership of the National Association for Writers in Education—NAWE—is good generally, but being a member of CAMRA if your pitching to a brewery or a pub chain is also relevant).
- Writing must be succinct and perfect in every way—this is the first example of your writing a potential client will get to see. Edited it well and ensure that every sentence is well crafted and needs to be there.
- Finally—why you? What makes you unique and special?

Your bio should:

- Include a brief pitch: The first few sentences should highlight who you are and what you do. For example, you might be a freelance copywriter with

expertise editing writing journals, or maybe you're a fashion blogger with 3000 followers. Keep it short—40–50 words is enough—and convince the reader you're the person for the job.
- Be relevant: Do your research and find out about the publication of company you're pitching to. There's no point mentioning your fashion blog if it's a gig writing for an electronics company; that's not going to impress them. However, that two weeks you spent working in your uncle's retail business selling electronic products, might give you enough credibility to make it to the shortlist.
- Be focused: Listing all your achievements since second grade means that the one's that just might interest the potential client are lost. Do your research. Understand the company. And focus in on your relevant skills and experience.
- Be positioned: What's the company about? Who is their ideal reader? What's their style and tone (look at some of their existing content)? By answering these questions you'll be able to write your bio is a style that sends out the message—you're just the person for them!

*Let's look at an example:*
This is the bio for Terri Morrison (a fictional freelancer, for the purpose of our demonstration!).

*Terri Morrison is a freelance content writer and blogger. She has experience writing in a variety of different fields, including retail, fashion and small businesses. Having freelanced for a number of years, she is comfortable handling multiple writing orders and only commits to schedules she is comfortable delivering to. As can be seen from the testimonials on her website, her client's requirements are paramount, and she ensures her writing is clear and consistent. Follow Terri on her blog or Twitter to keep up to date with her latest projects.*

Right away we can tell Terri is

- an *experienced* freelance content writer with happy clients,
- *specialised in* retail, fashion and small businesses and
- capable of *managing her own work.*

Want to add a personal touch? Here are a few suggestions:

*Terri is an irreverent copywriter and marketer. She's on a mission to stamp out yawn inducing posts and to make boring business blogs sparkle.*

*Terri is a freelance writer for hire, specialising in web content and blogging for small businesses and startups. She's also huge fan of WordPress, women's history, Star Trek and anything that screams geek!*

*Terri is an accomplished freelance writer, pro blogger, ghost writer and editor. Talk to her if you want to simplify content marketing, make more sales and make an impression in your market space.*

Depending on the industry and your own personal style, these might not be suitable—but they demonstrate that you can have a little fun with your bio, make it personal and still come across as a professional.

**Your social media profile:** Once you have a full bio, you'll need to turn that into something much smaller for social media. Here are some interesting examples we found online:

@sixthformpoet Please buy my book, I owe people money.

@JohnCleese Yes, I am still indeed alive, contrary to rumour, and am performing the silly walk in my new app thesillywalk.com.

@tomhanks I'm that actor in some of the movies you liked and some you didn't. Sometimes I'm in pretty good shape, other times I'm not, Hey, you gotta live, you know?

@MichaelACaruso I've learned I don't know anything. Have also learned that people will pay for what I know. Life is good.

@_PenelopeNYC Coffee-Drinker, eReader Addict, Mom, Blogger. I'm very busy and important.

@ohyesshecan social strategy & implementation. Will work for shoes.

@MargaretAtwood author.

@neilhimself will eventually grow up and get a real job. Until then, will keep making things up and writing them down.

@paulocoelho I delete tweets.

@jackiejcollins Kick-ass writer!

What works about these very short bios?

- They're humorous so immediately capture our attention
- They also link to something they want to promote (book, app etc.)
- They come across as human—even when rich and famous. We can even relate to Tom Hanks
- They're brief—they're much less than the 280 characters available
- They immediately tell us a little about the person so we can then decide if we want to follow them

Tips for your social media profile:

1. If it's Twitter, it needs to be short and snappy!
2. Try to have a little fun with it.
3. Try to be upbeat and positive.
4. Be humble—arrogance doesn't go down well (unless of course, you're Jackie Collins, and then you can get away with it).
5. Don't tell lies.
6. Reveal a little something about yourself, so that you come across as human.
7. Change it regularly.

**Open for business.** Now that you have a social media profile—advertise that you're for hire. Otherwise, prospects won't know if you have time to take on more clients plus it lets other freelance writers know that you are available for writing work.

## The Life of a Freelance Writer

*'The freelance writer is a man who is paid per piece or per word or perhaps.'*
Robert Benchley

Okay, Benchley's remark is pretty outdated now but his point is still valid—regardless of gender, it's a tough business when you want to turn your passion for writing into cold hard cash.

A good place to start is to get to know other freelance writers. It can be a pretty lonely world, sitting at your desk searching for some paid writing gigs when you first start out freelancing. One of the best things you can do is to network with other writers. They understand what you're going through and might even have some tips for you. Remember, we're all in this together—it isn't a competition. Conversations around going rates and typical hours are heathy discussions that more freelancers should be having—and it's in our interest to do so! Just like it is with buses—you can wait for ages for one to come along—and then suddenly you have more buses that you can handle. Well, so it is with freelancing. If you have a network of other writers around you, you can support each other and pass work on (just be sure they know their stuff, are suitable and reliable). It's great for the writers, and it's great for your clients. A win-win for everyone involved.

It's all too easy to glamorise the life of the freelance writers—sleeping in until midday, having coffees at the local café or lying around on their sofa with their laptops, writing what they enjoy and getting paid plenty for doing it. And of course, they work when they want, or just take the day, or week off!

I'm afraid we're here to tell you, it might be like that in the movies, but the reality is something else entirely. Okay, we might find the time to play the guitar, or go for a run, even spend time with the family. But there are a few home truths we're going to share with you.

The average day of the freelance writer: First of all, there is no 'average' day. Let's dispel this once and for all. A freelancer's day is going to vary greatly depending on what's going on….

**Rise and shine.** When you actually wake up might vary greatly, depending on your workload. If you're working for overseas clients, it's possible you're working late nights so you can fit in some important phone calls and meetings. So, you'll need to be flexible on this on, but definitely don't get into the habit of sleeping in. It will quickly eat into your working hours. And while we're on the subject of working from home—get up, get dressed and at least pretend you're going off to work. It's possible a client will catch you by surprise and want to have an urgent video call without notice. Trust me, you don't want to be caught out in your pyjamas and looking like you've not brushed your hair for a month.

**Allow time to look for writing gigs.** It's important to always keep the work coming in, even when you're busy with multiple projects, you'll need to be looking ahead for the next 3–6 months. Therefore, always allow for at least an hour to spend dedicated to finding work, looking for potential clients and sending off proposals.

**Administration.** This means checking emails and responding promptly. Within a few hours, if you can, even if it's just to say you'll need to get back to them shortly. But be careful; it's easy for this to become all consuming, so have a schedule and stick to it. I check my emails once in the morning and then once again in the afternoon. Rush to your emails everything you hear a ping (go and turn it off now, by the way) and you'll find yourself doing admin all day long.

**Kids.** Yep, they're a big reason some writers go freelance in the first place. It means you can schedule in your work around them. I often get up early so I can get a few hours in before the household awakes and then work when the kids are at school. The bonus is, I can be there for them when they need me.

**Make your own tea or coffee (and try to avoid the biscuits).** By this we mean that you need to allow time for breaks. It's good for your physical well-being (sitting at a desk for too long is good for no-one), but it's also vital for your mental health.

**IT support.** Alas this one is daunting for many freelance writers, but you will need to do it yourself. Or at least you'll need to find someone who can help you. The freelancer doesn't have an IT department to call on, so find someone reliable who can be a phone call away. It's important that you have a regular IT checklist. For example, you might be to have regular updates. And it will happen—you have an important piece of work to complete and your laptop dies. So, have a backup plan ready (such as that old laptop in reserve). And if you've got technical skills, keep yourself up to date and you'll save yourself a lot of support bills as well as time.

**Hanging out by the water cooler.** Okay, it's unlikely you can actually do this one, and even if you do happen to have a water cooler, it's probably just going to be you and the dog hanging out. But in all seriousness, you do need to keep in touch with others, who are sort-of like your colleagues (by this we mean, other freelancers). So do make sure you allow some time to catch up with your writing buddies. So long as you're meeting up for coffee to discuss work, and not daytime soap operas. Including a number of freelancers, will help avoid this happening.

**Be your own boss.** This means you have to organise yourself and crack the whip sometimes. No one is going to reprimand you for having a break and watching daytime television. In fact, you can do it all day if you wish. But it will mean you're not freelancing, you're not earning money, not are you working on finding work. So come up with a schedule, including writing targets, and then build in some down time.

**You're now the finance director.** Yep, you need to keep on top of your finances. There's no point working twelve-hour days writing, if you don't know if you're making enough to pay the bills. So, set aside time to work on your accounts. Make sure you have important dates in such as when tax returns are due, and allow yourself enough time to complete any necessary forms and so on.

**Meet clients.** When you're calculating the time it will take to complete a writing gig, ensure you build in 'non-writing' tasks. Taking time to speak with your clients is essential—beyond just reading their job brief. It means you can ask questions, clarify the details, and also get to know them. And it's important to give them a quick curtesy call afterwards, just to check they were happy with the job done, and if there is anything else you can do to assist them.

**Stay up to date.** It's all too easy to forget there's a world outside your office (or wherever it is that you work from). But allow time to keep informed on any developments in your field or area of expertise.

**Be your own personal assistant.** You need to manage your own diary, make sure you know what appointments you have that day and be prepared for meetings. You need to prioritise your time, so you can focus on what's important.

**Have a holiday.** This will likely be at a time when there's no work going. If you're smart, you'll try to plan your schedule around the busy periods and then have some well-earned breaks when it's quiet.

**Be your own personal trainer.** This means finding time to look after yourself. Without that person in the office who reminds you to get up and make the coffees, it's all too easy to sit at your desk and just keep working. Make sure you allow time to get some exercise, even if it's just taking the dog for a walk. Have a break for lunch, and don't eat it at your desk.

> **Top Tip**
>
> Working while on vacation—not a great idea. Your holiday companions are not going to appreciate it, and it's going to leave you just as tired. Holidays are a time to recharge the batteries. So, if at all possible, leave the laptop behind.

## Standing Out from the Crowd

First and foremost, clients are looking for great writers who can deliver the content they need. However, there's more to it than just your writing. Some ways to stand out include:

**Be a pleasure to deal with.** This means being obliging, friendly and helpful (even when the client is a right pain in the …). It's likely they probably under pressure and (unfairly) passing it onto you. They may not show their appreciation for your patience in their manner, but they may very well give you further work.

**Manners.** Yep, just like your mum always told you, good manners cost nothing and go a long way. And you'd be surprised how many people forget this. So, think twice before you write an email too quickly; pause and make sure you are being polite. If you make a mistake, that's okay, we all do from time to time. Just explain what's happened, apologise and provide options to rectify the situation.

**Be easy to work with.** Make sure you format your content for easy uploading and online readability. Provide your work before deadlines and ensure clients never need to chase you for an update.

**Be an outstanding communicator.** A good freelancer pays attention and asks questions. If they don't know something or aren't sure; they speak up. It's all about ensuring you really understand what your client wants and ensuring you can deliver exactly that. It's not about you interpreting the brief—it's about you *understanding* the brief. So, don't just think you know what they want. Go back and ensure that you have understood it correctly.

**Deliver the most up-to-date statistics and facts in your content.** We can all write churn, and by this, I mean searching the web and re-churning it out again. The same old same old content can become, predictable dull and boring. Make sure your content is vibrant and original, then you provide the added value that other freelancers don't—and crucial to this is topicality. Even casual cultural references, if you mention, Beyonce's "new album" *Lemonade* in passing you need to remember it came out in 2016 and isn't new any longer.

**Be professional.** You might work from home (and even in your pyjamas sometimes), but never forget that you're also a professional. That means you should always convey a professional image. Have a business email account—you can see how bigbadedie@homeville.com works with your friends and family but for business—well? Use a letterhead on your invoice. And also agree a work brief and rate *before* you start working.

**Be human.** We all make mistakes, get flustered when things don't go well and sometimes we have bad days. Our tip is don't just press send. Give yourself time to take a break, have a cup of tea, do some sit ups—anything that de-stresses—and then go back to it. Also, a client might be having a bad day, behave badly and so on, but give them the benefit of the doubt. If things don't improve, leave it until tomorrow. If they consistently behave badly, then find some other clients.

## Key Chapter Points

- If we want to find work as a freelance writer, then we need to be flexible. As we have seen in this chapter, there are plenty of roles available that have writing at their core. It's important to understand where your abilities and interests lie, so you can focus in on the roles you'd most enjoy. But for many of us, it means being flexible and prepared to move between roles, to be able to make a living.
- There is much work to be done, to ensure we're ready to market ourselves as Professional Writers. This means crafting well-written profiles, bios, collating a portfolio of our work and having business cards produced.
- If we want to make freelancing a paying proposition, then we need to be serious about it as a career choice. Such as we would with any job, we need to establish a working routine, ensure we look after our personal lives and health, and find support and help from others.

- We can make a good impression for many reasons—and it won't all be about our writing abilities. Talents can make us impress, but someone who delivers to the brief, to agree timescales and is a pleasure to work with, really shines. Clients want to work with people who are pleasant, engaging, good listeners and obliging. Want clients to come back? Make yourself that person who's a delight to work with and can be relied upon!

**Exercise 3.1 Write Your Freelancer Bio**
**First line:** Introduce you, what you do, and where you're from.
   **Add the facts:** What are your qualifications? Are you a graduate of a writing degree? Even if you're mid-way studying, it's still important to mention this as it shows you're committed to your writing. Were you the editor of the school paper? Have you had any fiction of poetry published? (Any writing publication is fair game for your first writer's bio.) If you have not been published it's okay to mention any current writing projects. Be honest: your bio should reflect your passion and commitment to the writing craft.
   **Experience:** If you don't have any 'professional' experience, it's okay to list any web-writing you may have done for e-zines, blogs and so on. This at least shows that you are an active writer.
   **Writing niche:** What do you love to write about? And what makes you qualified to write about it? If you have run several marathons and enjoy writing about health and wellness, mention it.
   **Something personal:** Don't write a book, but a unique fact about yourself will help your bio stand out. Appropriate humour is a plus (but it must be appropriate).

**Exercise 3.2 Social Media Profile**
Now turn your freelancer bio into a 30-word profile for your Twitter/Facebook/Instagram account.

# 4

# The Art of Communication and the Freelancer

In this chapter we will:

1. Consider why communication is an important feature for any creative writer and why it's so important when you're freelancing, including ways that you can improve your communication skills. It's something we all need to work on and regularly brush up on!
2. Explore how communicating in business is different from other forms of communication. There are expectations. So, to avoid unnecessarily causing affront or misinformation and knowing how to effectively convey your message is important.
3. Get very practical and cover some basic tips for your writing to make it more business-like and get your message across.
4. Get up, close and personal with the humble email. It's a fundamental form of communication, in all walks of life, but it's also a form that often gets misinterpreted. So, we'll discuss ways to ensure this doesn't happen.

'The single biggest problem in communication is the illusion that it has taken place.' George Bernard Shaw

Freelancing is primarily about people. We might be writing content, designing web posts, producing reports and so on, but to land the work, understand what is really required and establish lasting relationships with clients, it all comes down to people and good communication. You might be able to write the most amazing website content, delivery creative ideas, be an expert at your craft, but if you can't communicate with others, you'll never succeed.

# The Freelance Writer and Communication

When we say communication—it works both ways, between you and the customer, and the customer and you. It means you need to understand what the customer really wants (and this isn't always easy—they don't always communicate what they really want and indeed they are sometimes not sure what they need). But it is also about ensuring your messages are being received, not simply that the message has been sent. For example, when a client tells you that they want an all singing all dancing web page, telling them that will make the project very difficult and take a long time to deliver, isn't sufficient. You need to ensure they understand it will take ten additional days and result in content that will be much for difficult for them to maintain. Now we're putting it in their terms, what it will mean to them and any resulting implications. Time may not be critical to the client, and they are prepared to wait the additional days for features they consider important. But if time is critical you have to manage expectations. And of course, the additional workload of maintaining content could be addressed through training, or at a later date—which you can provide as an option. What's important is to let the client make that choice.

*Explain the implications—provide options—let the client decide*

When it comes to communication, great freelancers are instilled with a number of qualities (and don't worry, none of these are part of your DNA; they can be acquired):

**Patience.** Never talk down to someone or make them feel stupid or silly (even if they are being a bit stupid or silly). It's important to remember that they are experts in their own particular fields—I once wrote content for an air-conditioner installer—he didn't know anything about websites, but I know nothing about air-conditioners. Respect is fundamental to building long-term relationships and having clients that want to work with you in the future and will recommend you.

**Good listener.** Let people speak, ask loads of questions and make sure you have understood them correctly. Email is a tricky communication channel at the best of times, so it does no harm to say … I think this is what you mean / are saying / is this what you think you need. Also, and it's a good tip, let them talk about what they know about. Show an interest in them and they will show an interest in you. It's a bit like dating, really—and come on, we've all been there, the dates who just want to talk about themselves. But it's not a date, you're trying to get the gig, so show interest—both the date and the client will walk if you show disinterest.

Some tips to becoming a good listener include the following:

- Be an active, not passive listener. This means, take notes.
- Be attentive and focused on what the person is saying.
- Keep an open mind. You might think you know the best solution for the client but be prepared to try alternative approaches (especially if you want the gig).
- Listen to the words and try to draw a picture of what they are saying—if you can't picture it, then you need more information.
- Be patient—don't jump in too quickly. Let the other person finish what they are saying.
- Pay attention to the big picture and not just the small details. While something might seem a good idea in isolation, there are often wider implications to consider. The client will be impressed if your advice avoids a costly mistake. Or indeed your advice on a cheaper option works out for the best.
- Don't interrupt with your ideas/thoughts/solutions.
- Wait for the person to pause to ask any questions.
- Be relaxed—you'll hear more if you focused, attentive but relaxed.
- Pay attention to any non-verbals and what isn't being said.

**Available.** I once took a call from a client at 10 pm at night. He was in a major panic because he had a big presentation the following evening and couldn't get the proposal right. I put in a few hours work and he's still a regular client some ten years later. It's not something I'd do on a regular basis, but I knew the client and I realised he needed my help. These are calls you have to make (and take).

**Translators.** This means ensuring that clients understand the implications of any decisions. Rather than saying, you've included keywords to ensure maximum page traffic—explain what that actually means to them. Translate it into something tangible and real (maximum page traffic means more people will visit their website which means more potential customers).

**Empathetic.** Try to see the problem or the situation from the other person's point of view. Then restate what you have heard, just to be sure you really understand—especially before you make suggestions for improvements.

**Ask why a lot.** It's good to understand why the client wants something. Sometimes clients think they know the answer or solution to a problem, but it's wise to talk it through to clarify whether it will actually solve the problem.

**Upfront.** Explain what you will be doing (overview is fine) to ensure the client understands expected duration, complexity, costs and budgets. If there's a problem, identify the issue, determine options and then speak with the client. They might not like what you have to tell them, but they'll like it even less if they're expecting you to deliver it that day and you don't have the goods!

**Get to the point.** Clients (and hopefully you) are busy! They are talking to you about a specific issue, so don't ramble on with unnecessary details or chit-chat. Get straight to the point and be very clear about what you need from them.

**Stay in the loop.** Even if you're not working for a client, it's good to stay in touch. Check out their website, Twitter and so on just to ensure you remain fresh in their memory. Drop them a short email to say hi. Ask them how their business is going and if you have a suggestion for them, let them know.

**Discuss.** Do put forward options but remain open to the ideas and suggestions of others. And seek input. Don't be shy to speak up with suggestions—nobody knows everything, so do tell them if there is something they should know.

**Get help.** Knowing when to call in the assistance of others, is important. If the job is too big for one, have somebody you trust standing by—and hopefully they will return the favour at a later date.

**Own the job.** Even if you need help, once you have been commissioned the job is yours. Own it, nurture it, do it to the best of your ability, and if you engage someone else to complete a part of it, take the overall responsibility and do the final check before it goes to the client.

> **Top Tip: Set Standards**
>
> Set your own bar high and never let that standard slip. Shoddy work soon brings a reputation you don't need.

## How Does Communicating Professionally and Business-like Differ from Other Forms of Communication?

*Writing for business* typically has a specific purpose or goal. This is what makes Business Writing different from other forms of writing. For example, writing fiction is often about creating worlds where readers experience feelings (happiness, fear, loneliness, suspense etc.) It is a place for the imagination which is usually out of place in a professional document. With a business document, practical details such as information, times, objectives and actions are key. Emotions tend to have lesser importance and can distract from the objective.

That's not to say emotions don't play a role—a client might feel attached to a solution they feel is best (if when logic says it's not)—therefore in such situations, always stick to the facts. Show the client the implications of the solution they want—then give them alternatives—but ultimately, it's their decision. Your role is to inform them of the facts.

An *essay* often sets out to state a point of view and to support it with research and evidence. It may need to conform to specific requirements, such as word length, and answer a specific question. Academic writing is clear, concise, focused, structured and backed up by evidence. Its purpose is to aid the reader's understanding of a particular topic and has a formal tone and style.

Business communication and writing aims to *convey a message* and has a *specific objective* it wants to achieve. That might be to inform them that you've seen that their blog hasn't been updated in six months and you have some items for content. Or it might be to offer your services to write a report. There's an objective—very rarely do we send a business email just to say 'Hi!' And if you do, it's because that business associate has now become a friend, and it's a different type of communication. When we're writing for a business purpose, the aim of the writer is to propose plans or recommend actions that will benefit the recipient, and to do so as concisely as possible. And this is also a good reason to have a separate email address for business. Keep your personal and business life apart. Log onto your business account and go into business mode. I have a friend who is a journalist and novelist. He writes his novels on a desktop computer and his journalism on his laptop. This helps him to quickly get into the right mode for the task at hand.

Developing an effective business writing style is important for any professional writer. Just like you can recognise each of your friends from their emails before you even get to the end, it's likely that your business associates will do the same eventually. And what you really don't want is for them to go … 'oh no, another email from Andrew, and he's waffling on again!' Far better is, 'Ah, it's an email from Lisa; I know she only contacts me when necessary and she'll give me clear guidance on what she needs.'

Effective professional communication

- states the main point clearly and this is near the start of the document;
- includes all necessary information that is organised in a logical manner (excluding any unnecessary information);
- is concisely written, without any unnecessary words or details;
- is easy to understand, with short sentences and paragraphs; and
- is focused with active language and plain English.

> **Top Tip: Be Structured**
>
> Brainstorming is a great way to get ideas down and get started. But once you've got enough ideas down, it's time to add structure. Begin with groupings your ideas into sections (you might want to do this with post-it notes or online—the method is up to you) but once you can see your main sections, you can start to discard those ideas that are superfluous.

## Getting Your Message Across

There are various techniques and approaches we can apply to help make our writing more efficient, precise and convincing. In other words, more professional.

### Use Active Voice

'The brand *Green Pastures* conjures images of nature' is stronger than
   'Images of nature are associated with the term, *Green Pastures*.'

### Avoid Passive Voice

Using forms of the verb 'to be' (is, be, am, are, was, were, been)
   Passive: 'What the brand is missing is …'
   Active: 'The brand needs …'
   Passive: 'Conclusions have been drawn and recommendations have been made.'
   Active: 'The report concludes with recommendations.'

### Stick to Simple and Shorter Sentence Structures

'Realtime Solutions have conducted all necessary tests according to industry standards.'
   conveys a clearer message than
   'If product X is to sell well in Europe and eventually in selected global markets as well as to compete with distributors of similar products, the brand must confirm to industry tests, and accordingly Realtime Solutions have provided these.'

## Be Specific

'To achieve the target results, costs must be cut by 50%.'

And not: 'Due to changes in market demand, compounded by industry pressure, our target figures are under pressure. However, with some cost cutting we hope to meet agreed targets.'

## Be Positive But Curb Enthusiasm

Avoid exclamations marks and language and overly enthusiastic language such as thrilled, delighted and so on.

## Avoid Qualifiers

These are words or phrases that add nothing, and actually weaken what you are saying.

For example: 'It may be required …', 'The following recommendations might be considered:', 'We probably need to …'.

## Keep It Professional at All Times

Don't say: 'Did you watch the match last night?'

Instead, if you also have a personal relationship with the person outside of work, write a separate email (coming from your private email account).

## Write from the Point of View of the Company

For example, 'The company must change the name of its autumn range.'

And not: 'I recommend that the company change the name of its autumn range.'

## Write More Univocally

This is where the voice of the company is a social voice.

For example, 'The company must change the name of its leisure merchandise.'

And not, 'Even though Justine in the Finance and Mark in Sales disagree, the company must change the name of its leisure merchandise.'

## Avoid Nominalising Verbs

Nominalising is changing verbs into nouns, that is, 'decide' into 'decision'.

For example, 'The Project Manager decided to launch the project in Europe.'

And not, 'The Project Manager made a decision …'.

## Recommend Action Rather Than Refer to Individual Mental States

For example, 'We recommend names that parallel the image and funky qualities of the brand.'

And not, 'We believe you should use …', or 'We think …', 'We imagine …', 'We presume …', 'Why don't you …' and so on.

## Avoid Qualifiers That Weaken Recommendations Or Express Doubt

'We recommend that your company avoid the use of the word 'contamination"—this sends out a clear message.

Whereas 'We tentatively recommend that your company, if at all possible, avoid the use of the word "contamination"' is ambiguous at best.

## Avoid Personalising Pronouns, and Personalising Problems

'The company needs to …'

And not, 'You need to …'.

## Use the Imperative Voice

This is where you begin with a verb and assumes the subject 'you' for recommendations. The imperative voice is concise and eliminates the moral tone of 'should' and the overly emphatic tone of 'must'.

Examples: 'Balance work with the lives of employees'; 'Recognise the value of the senior leadership team'; 'Create self-managed project teams.'

## Use Verbal Rather Than Nominal Forms (Verbs Changed into Nouns Or Adjectives) of Words

Rather than: 'person-organisation fit issues' use 'Organisation policies fit employee expectations.'
Rather than: 'management-directed policies' use 'Managers direct policy.'

## Use Parallel Structure

These are phrases that repeat the same grammatical structure.
Rather than: 'The business

- has no defined future objectives or goals.
- is shortsighted without budget and long-term goals.
- has no reward system.
- does not appear prepared to respond to rapid changes in the industry.'

Use, with parallel structure: 'The business

- lacks defined objects and goals for the future;
- needs to agree short-term and long-term budgets;
- rewards merit only for individual production; and
- adjusts too slowly to industry forces.'

## Eliminate Unnecessary Words

Rather than: 'My suggestion is that we must begin to introduce our employees into the company culture. They can then begin to internalise the core values of lowering costs and increasing quality that aim to achieve.'
Use: 'Train employees so they will internalise the core values of the company.'

## Select Words in an Appropriate Register (Vocabulary and Tone) for Your Reader

If your message is aimed at the CEO, s/he doesn't need to be reminded by you of the organisational objectives. Nor do they want to hear a load of details.

## Provide Possible Solutions and Any Implications

A rule of thumb, the higher in an organisation you are communicating with, keep it brief, tell them what you need them to do, why it is necessary, and if going to them with a problem, don't expect them to solve it for you.

## Be Cautious with the Use of Jargon

If your email is to the IT Director, s/he'll be fine with IT jargon—not so the Director of Marketing or Finance. Be mindful of who you are communicating with and use appropriate language.

> **Top Tip: Remember—You Don't Know Where an Email Might End Up**
>
> Regardless of who in an organisation you are communicating with, always keep it professional. You just don't know where your email might end up! Emails can quickly turn into a chain of emails, and other people copied in. Also, people talk—I'm unlikely to be friends with someone who treats a waiter or waitress badly; you get the point.

# The Humble Email

There are many different forms of professional writing, and we don't intend to cover all the nuances of every different form. If you're writing a report, for example, there are many publications available on this and can provide you with detailed guidance. What is more useful is for you to have tips and hints that can apply to all of your professional writing, regardless of the form. However, there is one particular form that we think is extremely important, and that's the email. It may very likely be the first form of contact that you have with a potential client, so it's essential you get it right.

Emails allow us to communicate quickly and cheaply with colleagues, suppliers and other contacts across the globe. It has become the main means of communication in the workplace, yet typically, because it is viewed as less formal than a printed business letter, it tends to get much less attention. Given that, combined with the number of emails we all generally receive each day, it's fair to say that often our email messages do not always convey the message we'd hoped.

## Emailing for Success

To begin with, ask yourself, is email actually the best method to communicate? Very sensitive or highly personal information is better communicated in person. If physically in person isn't possible, consider a phone call. Is the information you want to tell the person likely to surprise them? If so, consider calling ahead to forewarn them of what is coming, or preface it with a short note.

Do you have the right person? If I receive an email that's addressed to 'dear Madam', I know the person hasn't bothered to find out my name and I move on; it's only taken me a split second to decide it's spam. It may not be, but I won't be reading it. So, take your time and find the right person who you think is responsible for what is required? What do you do if you don't get a response? Out of courtesy, inform the person before going to contact someone else.

Think about who should the communication be coming from? More often than not, it is from the person writing it but there can be instances where you are writing on behalf of someone else. If that's the case, make it clear.

Basic rules that can increase your odds of getting your message across:

- Take the time to write a good email and edit it. Just because emails are a quick method of communicating doesn't mean that you shouldn't take care with your writing.
- Edit check for typos, poor punctuation and mistakes.
- Consider the layout—a lack of white space makes it difficult to read. Break it up into short paragraphs. Adding structure will help your reader understand your message.
- A good rule to follow is one point or question per email. If you have more than one, it all too often happens that the person replies and misses some of your requests.

## General Email Etiquette

- It's tempting to fall into the trap of being informal as the email format is something we use so regularly. But it's essential to always keep work-related emails professional and friendly.
- Open and close an email using 'Dear' at the beginning and 'Best wishes' or 'Regards' at the end.
- 'Hi' is not appropriate for business emails unless you are familiar with the person you are writing to.
- If you do not know the person's full name, use their title (e.g. 'Dear Marketing Manager') or 'To whom it may concern' or 'Dear Sir/Madam'.
- A good rule of thumb: people are unlikely to be offended if you are too formal, but some may think you are being rude if you are too informal.
- Check the tone—when we meet people face to face, we use the other person's body language, vocal tone, and facial expressions to determine how they feel. Email robs us of this information with the result that we can't tell when someone has misunderstood our messages.
- Choice of words, sentence length, punctuation, and capitalisation can easily be misinterpreted without visual and auditory cues. And surely everyone knows, THIS IS SHOUTING IN EMAIL SPEAK—IT DOESN'T ATTRACT ATTENTION FOR THE RIGHT REASON; actually it reads like one those emails that says I'll send you $50,000,000 business proposals.
- It is never a good idea to add 'x' to your name when closing (unless it's your mum).

## Addressing an Email

- To—this is where you type the email address of the person you are writing to.
- CC (courtesy copy)—this is for the email addresses of other people who need to see the information in your email. Only do this if there are involved, will be affected by or should be informed.
- BCC (blind courtesy copy)—addresses that you put in this field are 'hidden' from the other people who receive the message. For example, if you wrote an email to your insurance company but wanted a solicitor to read it

for reference without the insurers knowing, you would use this field for the solicitor's address. Only use this if absolutely necessary, and it puts the BCC'd person in a difficult position and they know the content of the email, but the receiver isn't aware they do! Also, it's sometimes a good idea to BCC to your other account (of course you should have more than one), just so you can have a copy (we do this all the time). Servers go down, emails get lost, gremlins sneak in and do unspeakable things—it's a belt-and-braces job.
- Always use the correct field so people know who you expect to act first on the information.

## Subject Line

- Your subject needs to grab your reader's attention and summarise its intention, and a well-written subject line delivers the most important information, without the recipient even having to open the email. It also serves as a prompt every time they glance at their inbox.
- A blank subject line is more likely to be overlooked or rejected as spam.
- You may want to include the date in the subject line if your message is one of a regular series of emails, such as a weekly project report. For a message that needs a response, you might also want to include a call to action, such as 'Please reply by November 7.'

## Body of the Email

- Needs to be clear and concise.
- Keep sentences short and to the point.
- Should be direct and informative and contain all pertinent information.
- Focused—if you need to communication different topics consider having separate emails for each. This makes your message clearer, and it allows your correspondent to reply to one topic at a time.
- Check spelling and grammar—email applications have built-in checkers but don't rely on this.
- Avoid shortcuts of 'text messaging'. While some people may understand what 'cant w8 2 cu' means, a lot of people do not appreciate it.

## Some Examples

### Example 1

Hey Mike!
   Got your email. Was just wondering about a possible meeting—there's a few things I'm really not so happy about. No rush at all.
   Hey, did you see EastEnders the other night?
   Speak soon, if you want.
   Cheers,
   Dx
What's bad about this?

- The opening is too informal and impersonal, and the exclamation mark seems overly enthusiastic.
- The opening sentence is too casual, informal and unprofessional. And, crucially, there's no thank you for responding to the initial email.
- The second paragraph is a poor attempt at adding a 'personal touch'. As long as it's professional, courteous and polite, there's no need to throw anything like this in.
- The third paragraph is far too casual and indecisive, leaves too much room for doubt and suggests someone easily placated and generally not all that bothered.
- 'Cheers!' is best avoided, unless you've already developed a long-term relationship with the recipient. Even then, it's not ideal in a business capacity.
- Finish with both your full first name (at least) and a proper sign-off. This is far too casual and is what you might expect to see in a text message.
- 'x' is never good.

Better version:
Dear Mike
   I hope you are well. It was great to hear from you—thank you for your time yesterday.
   Could we set up a meeting to discuss the further? Let me know when's best for you and we can arrange something. It'd be great to discuss this in person, rather than by email.
   If you have any further questions on this, don't hesitate to ask. I look forward to speaking to you again.
   Kind regards
David

## Why Is This Better?

> **Example 2**
>
> Subject Line: New Product Releases
> Hi
> I was curious if you had any concerns about how your new products are hitting revenue goals or if you are trying to figure out what is and isn't working with your customers. I know first-hand how frustrating and challenging it can be to keep customers focused on your products, so your revenue goals are met…without busting your budget.
> We've had tremendous success with companies like ABC Corporation, where we drove 150% net new business, when we worked with XYZ Inc. we were able to reduce partner cost by 50% and we helped ACME Inc. close $1.2M in new business in 6 months.
> Would it make sense for us to chat? If you do not have any concerns about your products, then I want to respect your time and there would be no need to chat. If, however, you have areas you are trying to address, I'd like to learn what those challenges are. Would you be so kind to let me know if you feel quick chat would be valuable to you?
> Have a great weekend!
> **What's bad?**
>
> - Way too long—184 words
> - Opening sentence screams 'I want to sell you something'
> - No name
> - The email is all about the sender
> - Very weak call to action
>
> **Better:**
> Dear Mr Benson,
> I recently saw your new products on sale at ShedsAreUs. There are a couple of key techniques that will help you to leverage sales of these new lines.
> I have time on Wednesday afternoon or Friday morning to share these ideas with you. Would you have any time free on those days?
> Regards,
> Jennifer Townsend

- Subject line is relevant to the prospect's responsibilities, which were found on a quick Google search on the company.
- It is short and easy to scan—powerful 75 words.
- The call to action provides value and provides options of days to further discuss the possibilities.

## Bad Email Habits

- Sending an email as urgent that isn't.
- Putting words all in CAPS (unless you really want to yell at the person).
- Being too casual—think very carefully before using exclamation points, emoticons, abbreviations (such as LOL or BTW), slang, coloured text, fancy fonts, SMS shorthand or very familiar language.
- Avoid coming across as too formal—as though a robot rather than a human.
- Using an inappropriate email address from which to send your email (such as 'hotlips@googlemail.com'). If you do not have a business email address, set one up (use your name or your company name).
- Replying All.
- Sending emails to more than three or four people. If multiple people need to be included, make it clear who is required to take action.
- CCing without approval.
- BCCing (when the BCC'd person doesn't understand why they have been included—and it means they can't actually respond).
- Sending emails at odd hours (can create the wrong impression).
- Using a vague subject line or not including one at all.
- Bad grammar or poor formatting.
- Sending unnecessary replies (such as simply 'Thanks').
- Sending an email in anger. If it's possible an email is contentious leave it a couple of hours and come back to it. Sometimes a phone call might be more appropriate.

## Good Email Habits

- Be concise—aim for a maximum length of five paragraphs. For longer messages, consider sending the details as an attachment.
- Title the email clearly in the subject box and keep it short. This helps the reader to refer to your email at a later date.
- Use 'plain text' for your formatting rather than HTML (which creates webpage-style emails). This will mean that everyone reading your email will see it as intended. Bear in mind that not everyone uses a computer to access their email, and people may be using a device that can only display text.
- Use bulleted lists and keep paragraphs short.

- If sending pictures or documents with the email, make sure that they are a reasonable file size (less than 5MB) as big files can be problematic for the receiver. Always tell the reader that you have included an attachment.

> **Top Tip: Be a Prompt Emailer!**
> Always reply to an email as soon as possible. It shows the sender that you are dealing with the information (even if it's just to say that you will respond in full within 24 hours, for example). Plus, it quickly moves an item off your to-do list. We're not saying monitor your inbox all the time, but when reading an email, if you can address it in that moment, it will save you time to do so.

## Disclaimers

Many companies insist on using an email 'disclaimer' at the bottom of all their outgoing emails. There is some doubt as to how legally binding disclaimers are, but they can be used to inform the reader that the contents of an email are confidential. It's important to remember that a disclaimer doesn't mean you are not liable for any defamatory statements you make in the email.

## Signatures

Signatures should be kept short. Include name, company address and contact details. Avoid including product slogans or website links that are irrelevant to the content of your email. Also don't have 'meaningful quotations' when writing business emails. As they can seem pretentious and won't necessarily convey the right image of the company. Also, don't litter your signature with unnecessary qualifications—most of which won't matter. It's of no relevance that Lisa Kesteven could be referred to as Dr Lisa Kesteven, BBus, BA, DCA, and Andrew Melrose as Professor Andrew Melrose BA, DPhil.

# Key Chapter Points

- A successful freelance writer is an outstanding communicator, and this begins much earlier than when they start writing. Good communication skills are much more than writing—they include being patient and listening

to your client so that you truly understand what they want. It's being able to express yourself and convey the message you need to say.
- Establishing strong communication skills in all aspects of your professional life will ensure that you build good working relationships and are able to deliver what is required.
- Finessing your writing skills will ensure that you're clear in your message and less open to misinterpretation. Writing for business is different to other forms. It's much less about creative use of language or our huge vocabulary. It's about ensuring we're getting the message.
- Emails are fundamental forms of communication, which many of us rely upon. It's very likely that you'll never meet a client in person; that they are very busy and little time for phone calls. Therefore, you may need to rely on this electronic form of communication. Take your time and ensure it's well written—and always check for typos, especially with predict-text on (we have seen some howlers—and sent them, if we are honest).

## Exercise 4.1
*The Local Government Association (LGA) in the UK has published a list of 200 banned words (we've included them in the Appendix, so you can see them for yourself). It's a useful reference that covers many of the worst examples of poor use of English. So instead of saying 'working together', councils and public bodies refer to 'collaborative working', 'benchmarking' is used instead of 'measuring', 'outcomes' instead of 'results' and 'funding streams' rather than 'money'. And as the LGA says, horrendous terms like 'mainstreaming', 'contestability' and 'pathfinder' have no real meaning at all and should be scrapped altogether.*

If you could abolish 20 words or phrases, which would they be?

To get you started, here's some that would definitely make our list:

- At the end of the day
- Blue-sky thinking
- Can I ask
- Capacity building
- Framework agreements
- Going forward
- If I might say
- Place shaping
- Transformational
- Value-add
- Worklessness

**Exercise 4.2**
You've been commissioned to write an article for a hiking boots retail website, on a local mountain range. Only you've done some research and discovered that a competitor brand did a very similar article over a few months previous.
What do you do?

1. Forget you saw it. It's a paying gig after all, and you really need the cash. They should have done their research. It's their fault!
2. Tell them what you found and offer them a couple of other ideas for potential articles.
3. Tell them what you found but say that your article will be far superior.

Discuss each option and the pros and cons of each—firstly, for the client, and then secondly, for yourself, the freelancer.

# 5

# Writing for an Online Market

In this chapter we will:

1. Be going online and discussing how writing is different when it's for an online / digital market.
2. Discuss how each business/client will have their own distinct style and image. It's essential we know what this is, and we write accordingly.
3. Consider an online market.
4. Reflect on how readers behave differently online, so it's important that our writing reflects this.

*'On the average Web page, users have time to read at most 28% of the words during an average visit; 20% is more likely.'* Nielson Norman Group (https://www.nngroup.com/articles/how-little-do-users-read/)

*'The average attention span of Internet user has dropped to 8 seconds as compared to 12 seconds in 2000 and 55% of all page views get less than 15 seconds of attention. Web users spend 69% of their time viewing the left half of a page and 30% viewing the right.'*
   How People Read Content Online—Statistics and Trends, 25 June 2018 (https://www.go-gulf.ae/how-people-read-content-online/)

# Writing for Digital Media

Many of the elements of good writing apply whether you're writing for an online audience or an in-print reader. However, the approach to writing differs when we go online. We must take into consideration the simple fact that readers behave and 'read' online content very differently. As we can see by the statistics above, online readers don't hang around. They browse, snatch at something then move on, browsing again, clicking here, clicking there, moving on... Look at your own 'browsing history' after just an hour of looking around! If our online writing is going to have a strong impact, which it needs to do if anyone is going to read it, we have to approach our writing very differently.

There's no denying it's easier to get your writing published online than it is in print. However, there are some very important differences:

- Your online words may very well remain online for a very long time—and any 'sub-standard writing' might go on to haunt you once you're a famous author.
- It's easy to disappear amongst the volume of online content. Only the best will standout and really have any impact. So, ask yourself, does it stand out, and if not why?
- It's instantaneous. Unlike more traditional printing, it's very possible your copy will be made live without it being thoroughly edited. Many small businesses rely on you to provide clean and checked copy. They don't have the time or staff to check copy and will sometimes post copy with little more than a quick scan.
- Some online formats, such as Twitter, are very fast paced. If a reader follows numerous accounts, it's very possible that they blink and miss it. But also, how many times can you get away with a poorly worded or even downright silly post on behalf of your client—'Great news, my sister is pregnant, I can't wait to see if I'm going to be an uncle or an auntie ....'

The demand for online content in business is 'big business'. It must be kept fresh and up-to-date and, if the business is to stay ahead of the competition, it needs to stay relevant to the readership. Customers want content that is informative, useful, value add, entertaining and regular—and if a website doesn't provide what they demand, they'll simple go elsewhere. What they don't want is downright confusion or silliness. Though it's a big enough marketplace that there's a fair chance they'll find it—but not from you. What your client wants from you is valuable content that is leading edge and provides that something more, that their competitors don't have.

If a company doesn't have a website, then there's a good chance they're missing out on customers and potential sales. Website copy introduces online readers to the brand and their products/services. Carefully produced printed catalogues have been replaced by online versions. Potential customers can browse and look online at any hour of the day or night—and when they do, they expect quality. If content is done well, it will hook them in and turn them into a customer, but if it fails to do so, more often than not, the customer will move on, in search of that website that does meet their needs. Put yourself in that position—did you ever hang around in a website that was just wasn't a pleasure to browse? It's no different from a good book or magazine, if we don't like it, we cast it aside. But it's also important to remember the site has to 'keep' those browsers, so regular content doesn't regurgitate the same old information—it offers the reader something new and interesting each time, providing them something of value. Think of how many times you actually return to a website—it needs to be offering something that stands out and is extra special, to draw you back.

Search engine results and page position is obviously key to driving readers to a website, and to create a sustainable and long-lasting ranking, search engines will look for high-quality content alongside high traffic. So, the writer's job is to keep bringing people to the content by making it good.

But what do we mean by website copy? This can include a huge variety of items—features about the company, its employees and customers, articles about new products, features on related items; for example: if you have a website selling products for dogs, regular articles on caring for dogs would be a value add to any dog owner—or even if you are promoting a lifestyle, blog posts, news and industry items, product page updates, company announcements… we could keep going. But take a look at this, https://www.boden.co.uk/en-gb/environmental-impact#nav—here we have a company highlighting the fact they are 'Reducing their environmental impact through responsible sourcing and packaging'. Ask, why are they doing this? Well, they will probably reply it's because they care but bear in mind it's also because their customer demographic cares. The customer knows they are perusing wares from a responsible firm, it fits their lifestyle so they can be persuaded to spend with an ethical conscience. Everyone's a winner—now who sang that? You're probably getting the idea that a company website has *a lot* of content, and it needs to be frequent and regular. Gone are the days where businesses had printed-off catalogues and produced guides—more often than not you'll find these online—creating an opportunity for the savvy writer to provide the written text to accompany the product images. And it has to be fresh and up to date. Mentioning sustainably sourced cotton can be as informative as the price—which isn't the only fact in a shopping transaction. This is especially the case when shopping online. An online company like Boden promote themselves as a lifestyle choice.

We've established there's a need, but how do you go about providing quality online copy that businesses will bite off your arm for?

## The Style Guide

Consistency is important and a style guide provides a uniform experience for the online reader. It outlines the basic standards that ensure any written or visual work have the same 'look and feel'. These standards generally include items such as grammar and punctuation, and often address structural elements of layouts, typography, citations and visual design. It might tell the writer the minimum words to use or that an image should be of a specific size. They can also specify rules for tone and voice.

If you're about to start writing for a business, check if they have any in-house style guides. If not, you'll need to build your own and even build one for them. Even if you establish a few basics, you can tweak them for each client you work with:

- Is it written in British or American English? And of course, this makes a difference—do you sell chips or French Fries; is it rubbish or garbage; petrol or gas (gasoline); a flat or an apartment; mobile or cell phone; crisps or chips; colour or color; centre or center; metre or meter; analyse or analyse; offence or offense; traveller or traveler—doing your own checklist would be fine, but actually you could just set your computer (though don't forget to change or vary it accordingly). If you become a competent writer in British and American English then you've also increased your potential job market—and with so much work online, there's no reason to limit yourself.
- Do they use abbreviations? Particular terms or language (e.g. if there in the IT industry they may use technical terminology).
- Tone (formal, casual, relaxed, friendly?)
- Typical paragraph length
- If writing blog posts—typical length?

A good starting point is The Writer's style guide available online and as a free app—www.thewriter.com/what-we-think/style-guide/

In the United Kingdom consider *The Oxford Style Guide* and *Copy-Editing: The Cambridge Handbook for Editors, Authors and Publishers*. Newspapers such as *The Guardian, The Observer* and *The Telegraph* have style guides available online. The BBC News also have one available via their website. This goes for any writer in any country. If you are reading this in Australia, the ABC (Australian Broadcasting Commission) has their own style guide. In the United States, there is the *New York Times Manual of Style and Usage*, which was first published in 1950. So, these are really helpful—even if you're not writing specifically for this outlet—as they provide general style information for specific countries and media.

The *Associated Press Style Guide* or the *AP Style Guide* is the recommended one for US journalists and can be used for online writing. It is a widely followed standard as it allows newspapers to easily sell or exchange stories without having to make wholesale changes in the press piece.

The Chicago Manual of Style on the other hand is equally well known but followed by authors and writers. It has updated social media guidelines for the digital age.

## Digital Platform Choice

Social media is big business, even if you're a small business, but in our experience and through our research we know people need help—not just with the technical aspects but with writing regular content and keeping up with demand. Also, they want to get on with what they are good at in the business, and if someone was to come along offering help, there's a good chance they are going to be interested. Unless a business has a social media team (and most small-to-medium businesses won't) it's likely they will need to limit their social media activity to one or maybe two platforms. It's up to the freelancer to help, to bring new and fresh ideas and also sometimes to curb their enthusiasm—as Albert Einstein once wrote on a blackboard, *not everything that counts can be counted, and not everything that can be counted counts*. While it might seem like a great idea to have a presence on every single platform going, trying to maintain this effectively can turn into a huge overhead. Start small and get a strong profile going on one platform, before considering another.

**Step 1. Choose the right platform.** If a business doesn't want to be tweeting at least a few times a week, then Twitter isn't for them. A blog might be more appropriate. Who are they trying to reach out to? If its teenagers, then LinkedIn isn't the way to go—perhaps something like Snapchat, WhatsApp, Facebook, TikTok, Instagram and YouTube will reach more of their target market—though by the time this book reaches you there may be more platforms in the making, it'll be up to you to monitor this.

**Step 2. Decide on the type of content.** For example, Twitter's character limit is 280. An SMS text message limit is 160. Pinterest pins can have up to 500 characters which increases the importance of writing succinctly. Facebook has unlimited word count and while it pretends to be used more for friends and family to keep in touch—it has become an increasingly aggressive advertising tool and it can be used for business purposes. LinkedIn is definitely a more professional social media platform, often viewed as an online CV. YouTube is one of the biggest search engines in the world. Not only that, but videos are on the rise. They are a fantastic way to catch someone's attention cue, Justin Bieber. Instagram too, who would have thought the idea of 'influencers' would become such a big deal even a couple of years ago? Rupi Kaur, the poet, has nearly four million Instagram followers; start following her yourself and see how it influences the 'advertisements' you get in your own Instagram account. Once again—do the research.

## Creating Scannable Content

Reading online is very different to reading a book or magazine. In the case of the later, we're less inclined to skip words or content because we might miss out on key information. Perhaps we're more invested in the reading (for example, we're purchased the book). When we read online there is much less investment and we're far more likely to skim read. We might jump between sections, scanning for details were interested in. It's not about reading content but quickly scanning through content to determine if it's what we want. We might jump around, taking in subheadings to see if it's worth pursing further. All too quickly we'll assess if it's interesting, if not we're off to another page. If we think of reading a novel as sitting down to a three-course meal, we'll start with entree… in this instance, reading online is more like a smorgasbord and we might just start with dessert! We are driven by two things: Does the website offer what we're looking for? And can we find it easily?

**In-demand content provides value.** This might be with useful information, insightful ideas and perhaps actionable tips. The more valuable and useful the information, the more likely the internet visitor is to return.

While you can't change your writing to make it more scannable, there are changes you can make to the overall format, which will help:

**Catch your reader's interest.** Address your reader directly and use the word 'you'.

**Have a WOW headline.** You have about three seconds to grab your audience's attention with a headline. If it's confusing or ambiguous, they'll simply stop reading and go elsewhere. Remember what we said about Salman Rushdie right at the very beginning. 'Naughty but nice' captures a lot. Aim for clear, succinct and tight your headlines, which capture attention and are informative.

**Have a WOW headline but it needs to be literal.** They might be boring and you're probably extremely witty and capable of coming up with very clever headlines but I'm afraid that's all wasted on Google and other search images. SEO (Search Engine Optimisation) needs literal—*Polly put the kettle on* might sound fun, but an SEO doesn't get your jokes or understands your clever workplace. So, keep your headlines simple and clear.

**Include an introduction.** Keep it brief—two or three key points that will be covered in your piece.

**Signposting.** Ploughing through pages of dense text is daunting. Readers like to have places to pause, and subheadings help give them a breather. They also help them navigate to the sections they're interested in.

**Use subheadings.** If you change a topic in your article, add a new subheading. This are signposts for your readers, and they can jump to the sections they are interested in. Search engines also use subheadings, so these can help with an article's SEO (Search Engine Optimisation).

**No more than four to six ideas.** Any more ideas and have a second, part two article. Don't try to cram too much content into your piece. With four to six ideas, aim to have one paragraph per idea. Your paragraphs don't have to be of equal length, but it's important to split up your ideas into separate paragraphs that are in bite size chunks for your readers.

**Most important point first.** At the beginning of your copy, tell the reader why they should take the time to read your piece.

**Stay focused and on topic.** Online visitors won't trawl through a lot of information to find what they're looking for. If there's a lot to cover, have several pages with links between.

**Write shorter paragraphs.** Long paragraphs are difficult to skim, and multiple paragraphs together only add to the reading complexity. Whereas short, sharp paragraphs of only a few lines, four sentences max, are much easier to consume. Include some white space (blank lines) and it becomes much more of a pleasing read.

**Bullet points.** These are useful for adding white space and can help to provide emphasis on key words, or to break a piece into sections.

**Use jargon with care.** Depending on who the intended audience is, you might need to provide explanations. Also be very careful with jargon. It dates very quickly and sometimes trying to be cool just isn't.

> **Top Tip: Use Plain English**
>
> The aim is not to impress people with your amazing grasp of the English language. It's about enabling your target audience to understand your message and then act upon it. Clean, clear and straightforward writing is best.

## Copy People Want to Read!

Make your copy a delight to read—this means removing unnecessary words, repetition and ambiguous terms. Shorten your text, so that your readers can easily understand your meaning. Don't overuse meaningless buzzwords or technical jargon. Unless your topic is extremely niche and technical, aim for about a *ten-year-old*. The average reading age of the UK population is that ability normally expected of a *nine-year-old*. This isn't a precise science; readers of *The Guardian* have the reading age of an average *14-year-old* and *The Sun* has a reading age of *8*. So, you are looking at addressing the *Love Island* (2020), *I'm a Celebrity Get Me Out of Here* (2020) demographic—or the popular shows of your day if you are reading this well after we wrote it. But the point is made, surely?

**Open with your important information.** Unlike an essay which begins with an explanation of what you're going to discuss, anything on the web needs to do the reverse. It opens with your most important points. Your reader isn't going to hang around, so don't waste time or space—tell them exactly what's key. It might be providing details of products or services, it might be important facts or background information, it could be an interesting development. Your readers want to know what you can do for them.

**Keep it short, sharp and simple.** On the web it's rare that a reader is seeking out creative and clever writing—they simply don't have the time. Simple statements often work best. Remember short paragraphs with four sentences max, and three to five lines at most. Use short sentences (around 12 on average). Shorten your text and skip unnecessary qualifiers, adjectives and adverbs, over-complex words and needless repetition.

**Active rather than passive content.** Active voice helps create succinct and engaging sentences. It's also more direct when you speak directly to the audience: 'You can do it' is more engaging than 'It can be done.' Also avoid questions like 'Is this what you're looking for?' Rather say, 'We have just what you need …….'

**Paint a picture.** Visualising something can help your reader understand. Generalities and high-level statements don't tell your reader anything.

Whereas, if you are specific and provide examples your reader will better understand and visualise your messages. Consider these two descriptions: This is the best dog toy money can buy—Or: This dog toy is made from durable, 100% natural material. It resists punctures and tears, even from the most dedicated chewers. Specific, descriptive product information also aids your website's SEO.

**Less is more.** Unless your client is particularly after something longer (let's say they have asked for a length essay on a particular topic—then stick to their brief), otherwise try to get as much value as you can out of your word choices. It can be hard to write less, especially when there is plenty you could say. So, don't waffle and stick to short sentences.

**Leave them wanting more.** Good webpages end with a call to action. Who should contact for more information? Is there an interesting video to watch? A related blog post or report to download? This strategy helps direct readers to other areas of the website and encourages them to promote content to their friends and family. Keep any calls-to-action succinct, and begin them with action verbs like 'download', 'share', 'learn more', or 'watch'.

**Know your keywords for SEO.** It's important to include keywords if you want to drive traffic to the website but don't keyword stuff. This negatively impact the readability of your content, its conversion rate and how well it ranks in the SERPs (Search Engine Results Pages).

**A dictionary is your friend.** If you're not sure of the meaning of a word, check it. Likewise, with grammar and spelling. And please, please, please don't rely on spell and grammar checks in Word for anything except the basics. Watch out for key words such as email versus e-mail, internet versus Internet, and Web site versus website versus web site. Technically all are acceptable but according to the *AP Stylebook* it is email, internet and website.

**White space.** By this we mean blank lines and lists (with a section of white space alongside). Visually this helps the reader take in the content. Pay attention to how good pages 'look'—read them like a designer. Long paragraphs can be overwhelming so add in some white space. Writing content for an online audience needs to bear in mind a number of things:

- Online readers scan—and they only read when they find what they're looking for.
- Visually it needs to be appealing.

**Don't forget your content might be read on mobile devices.** Anyone who has tried to read a long article on a small screen, and experienced the angst involved, will appreciate your efforts to format for a mobile device.

**Hyperlinks.** It's good internet etiquette to hyperlink back to a website if you reference another site's content. If concerned about sending traffic way to another site, choose 'open link in another window'. Sites will often reciprocate and link back when appropriate, so it's worth it to be polite.

It's not just new pages that need consideration. Every single page on a website should link to other pages. This helps boost rankings of the pages that are linked to, but it also encourages readers to move around the site. So, it's important to revisit older pages/posts and add in new links.

**Use restraint.** Use italics, boldface, underlining, upper-case type, asterisks, and changes of font or type size sparingly. Too much variety can leave the impression the writing is complex and confusing. Eliminate unnecessary clutter, such as unnecessary periods at the end of items in a list, as this isn't adding anything.

**Highlight important text.** If you need to draw attention to important material, try to make it stand out visibly, such as placing a border around the text.

**Professional quality means editing your copy.** If you can, do get someone else to edit your work. No writer is their own best editor. But if that's not possible, take a break between writing and editing. A day or two if you can, but at least several hours.

> **Top Tip: Keep Revisiting Posts**
>
> There is no such thing as a 'set it and forget it' content strategy. Analysing webpage stats such as social shares, pingbacks and web traffic is valuable information. But also monitor content for the keywords it's currently ranking for. Revamp posts with added content, updated info and a strengthened keyword strategy.

## The Visual and Verbal, Alongside the Written

A picture, or infographic or video, can often say much more than words. An easy-to-read chart can often do a better job of explaining a complex topic than text alone. Images also help break up text, making a page easier to read.

**Visual aids are appealing.** Things such as lists, tables, photographs, diagrams and graphs all add interest to a page and work towards capturing a reader's attention. Sometimes an image—say, a graph showing a decline in sales figures—will have a far great impact than it said in words. But these visual aids can also break up your text. When considering including photographs and images, ensure these support the topic / point and add additional value to any accompanying the text. An irrelevant or distracting picture might detract from the piece or leave the reader wondering why it was included. We mentioned 'sustainable cotton' before, see what this says, and how, https://www.whitestuff.com/sustainable-cotton/ look at the images as well as the clean lines and white space.

## Assessing and Evaluating Online Copy

It's important to be able to assess and evaluate your own copy as well as that of others. Strong copy goes beyond well written text. It also includes the formatting and display, and ensuring it conforms to any site tone and standards.

Here are some questions you can ask:

- Is the copy succinct but informative?
- Does the copywriting style suit the website's purpose and 'speak' to its target audience?
- Are bodies of text broken into easy-to-read chunks?
- Can text be resized through the browser or do CSS settings restrict size alteration?
- Is the contrast between text and its background colour sufficient to make reading easy on the eyes?
- Is text broken into small, readable sections and highlighted using headings, subheadings, and does it emphasise features where appropriate to assist in skimming?
- Within articles, are there links to more detailed explanations of subjects, or definitions of jargon terms?
- Is there an '"About" page' that identifies the author of the content?
- Does the copy credit any sources for content that was not written by the site owner?
- Have any testimonials been included on the site?
- Is the content regularly updated and doesn't live by the phrase 'set it and forget it'?

## Key Chapter Points

Want to make sure your online copy hits the mark?

- **Grab attention**—capture the reader's attention.

- **Ignite interest**—engage readers with unusual, counter-intuitive or fresh info. It might be raising awareness to a problem or describing advantages in a solution.
- **Spark their desires**—help them to make up their mind that they want what you're offering. It might solve a problem or offer some potential. Whatever it is, they desire it.
- **Prove**—convince your readers it's wise to act because what you're saying is true. You can achieve this through testimonials, endorsements, statistics, data and so on.
- **Action**—encourage them to take the next step.

## Exercise 5.1

Install *The Writer's* style guide or use their website
http://www.thewriter.com/what-we-think/style-guide/
Style Guide Quiz

- What is Flesch-Kincaid?

    A disease
    Readability tool
    Grammar checker

- Is it?

    Email
    email
    e-mail

- Exclamation marks:

    Two or three are okay, but don't go overboard
    Should be avoided
    Great for showing enthusiasm

- Do you write an email address as?

    thewriters.com
    http://www.thewriters.com
    www.thewriters.com

- An event is once every two years. Is it?

    Biannual
    Biennial

- For a UK phone number, is it written as?

    (01234) 567890
    01234 567890

## 5  Writing for an Online Market

- For a British and international audience, is it written as?

    +44 20 7940 7540
    +44 (0)20 7940 7540

- What's better?

    Therefore
    So

- Is it?

    Ten kg
    10 Kg
    10 kg

- Is it?

    Ok
    OK
    Okay

- Is it?

    Ie
    i.e.
    For example

- Job titles should be in:

    All capitals
    Lower case
    First letter in capitals

- Bullet lists should have punctuation at the end of each line

    True
    False

- Is it?

    Straight away
    Straightaway

- Ampersand (&)

    Can be used to reduce length of copy
    Don't use unless part of a name

- In American English, it's always 'dependent':

    True
    False

- Titles of books are written as:

    'The Oxford Dictionary'
    The Oxford Dictionary
    The Oxford Dictionary

- Is it?

    1000
    One thousand
    1,000

- A foreign word in common usage should be written as:

    Cliché
    Cliché
    'Cliché'

- If you're not sure you're talking about a man or a woman, do you use?

    They
    She
    He

# 6

## Self-promotion

In this chapter we will:

1. Discuss that being a freelance writer means that we don't just write for a living, but we also promote ourselves and our services. It's no good being a fantastic writer if no one knows it. We need to market ourselves to the right audience at the right time. This is an aspect that many of us aren't that comfortable with—but being freelance means we have to let people know that we're a writer and that we're worth them engaging our services!
2. Consider why we need an online presence (by that we mean a website and using social media). We'll give you lots of practical advice and tips for using online platforms efficiently and effectively.
3. Explore the freelancer's profile and how to make this stand out from the crowd (let's face it—there are lots of other writers out there competing for work, so we need to get noticed).
4. Look at how to build and maintain an effective freelancer's portfolio.

> Writing is like sex. First you do it for love, then you do it for your friends, and then you do it for money. Virginia Woolf

Being a great writer sadly isn't sufficient to make a successful career as a freelance writer. And let's face it, freelancing as a writer means—as Virginia Woolf so aptly puts it—we want to make money. We might write for the love of it but if we're going to making a living from our writing, we need to turn those words into an income (and we mean enough of an income to make it a viable proposition). To achieve that means self-promotion—letting people know you are out there and available to write.

# Becoming an Expert Self-marketeer

Writing content for other businesses is a good way for a freelance writer to earn a living. As we mentioned in the previous chapter, valuable content helps a company grow, promote their brands and make sales. But while a freelancer can become expert at marketing and promoting others, they often forget that they also need to promote themselves. And let's face it, if you're not promoting yourself well, clients will begin to wonder—you're offering writing as a service, so they'll be looking for examples of your craft, testimonials and endorsements—and that also means paying attention to your own self-promotional material.

There's a lot of competition because it is a global industry. Only recently we were approached with an offer from India. If a freelancer doesn't provide a quality service, the customer will quickly move onto the next available person and there are many who will happily step into your shoes. Therefore, it's crucial to remember that quality service means a lot of things—certainly you'll be an excellent writer (in the eyes of the client, not your own, by the way), but you have to be an outstanding listener, a diplomat, a planner, an organiser, a saint (with the patience of)—we could go on. A freelancer writer has to have a lot more skills than just writing. A big part of her/his success is self-promotion and convincing others that you're the right person for the gig. To be a successful freelancer you need to be able to work independently, both in juggling multiple work projects alongside ensuring there is a steady flow of work coming in, while maintaining your stamp of success for others to see.

But first and foremost, potential clients need to find you. This means advertising your freelancing services.

Having a website is a good start and shows the world that you're serious about freelancing. Having a wow website tells your potential customers that you know your stuff and deliver quality products. It's likely you'll also have profiles on job websites that describe your services. It's important that any sites that promote you as a freelancer are up to date and regularly maintained with portfolios of your work that show what you can offer. A fresh portfolio—which means up to date too—demonstrates the capabilities of the writer and what they're capable off. It doesn't show everything—it's just a taster.

Building trust and demonstrating your expertise are key to becoming a successful freelance writer. The more expertise you acquire in a subject, the more enticing you are to a client in that sector, and they will trust your content and want your services. These two qualities are built up over time, through examples of your work and by being active online. Participating in forums on social media, publishing blogs on high-profile sites and answering questions in your area of expertise, all help to build your profile as an expert. But you can also attend and participate in conferences and other industry events.

There are also some simple ways to ensure you're promoting that professional image that says: I'm a freelance professional writer and I know my stuff!

## Have a Website Dedicated to Your Freelancing Writing

This is a website where potential customers can view your work and is a must for any professional freelance writer. It might be tempting to have one general website under your name—highlighting all the weird and wonderful things you can do. However, if you're serious about becoming a freelance writer, don't be tempted to go down this path. It makes you appear as though you're dabbling and don't take your writing seriously enough to make it a career. There are plenty of templates available, try Wix, Blogger or WordPress. They are free and easy to set up.

> **Top Tip: First Impressions Count!**
> If your website appears professional, then that's the impression you'll leave with potential clients. Sadly, if it's poorly designed, outdated or simply not very appealing—that's what's the client will think of you and your work. You wouldn't go for that big interview in your old jeans, now would you (you wouldn't, would you?)?

A freelance writer's website should include:

- information about what type of writing services provided—for example, writing blog posts, website content, reports, editing, proofreading and so on;
- industries on which the writer has expertise—for example, retail, IT and sports;

- samples of work (just a one-page snapshot is fine—don't give away content which is valuable);
- a blog (optional, but a good idea!);
- credentials;
- testimonials; and
- how to contact (and make sure you follow up on enquiries within 24 hours).

Once you have a website, that's only the beginning—you'll need to promote it. Don't forget to include the link to your website on all your social media profiles. You can also use it as a part of your signature in every email you send and on your business cards:

For example: Cathy Kettle
Email: C.Kettle@writerforrent.com
Website: www.WriterForRent.com
Blog: WriterForRent.Blogspot.com

Twitter: No! Avoid it! At least from your professional self. The last thing you need is clients getting to know how you feel about the prime minister, last night's television and so on. And there is no point in saying you wouldn't be tempted. Even the former president of the United States got snared, and, as we write, hasn't the world's most popular author, J.K. Rowling, just managed to get caught up in a controversial debate which chipped away at her popularity?

## Blogs

A writer establishes their credibility through writing (no surprises there), so it's important to be regularly writing—even if you're not getting paid gigs. A good way of doing this is to be writing blog posts on a consistent and regular basis. These can then be added to the writer's blog, submitted to your social media platforms or offered for publication to other blogging sites.

Always include ways for potential clients to contact you, such as providing a link to your website, your email address and links to your Twitter and Facebook accounts. The objective is to build up a following, and if enough people know you're a good writer and available for work, there's a good chance enquiries will follow.

If you're struggling for ideas on what to write about, consider:

- writing about subjects you have some expertise in;
- writing about projects you've been involved in (if you can't use their details, keep it anonymous);

- providing advice on your own freelancing experiences; and
- focusing on the craft of writing—your writing techniques, your daily routine, tips and hints.

## Forums

Forums are another very effective means of self-promotion as well as a great way to network with other freelancers. You may hear about businesses and individuals looking for writers, and at the same time pick up tips. Or you might visit forums for website owners or companies looking for writers. It's an opportunity to discuss your content writing ability and your expertise with SEO optimisation. Your signature post should always include a link to your website.

# What Are You Good At?

## Identifying Your Strengths and Weaknesses

What you're good at might seem an odd question but when just starting out, and it can be tempting to bid for all and every piece of work going. Especially when first joining freelance work sites and seeing work for offer, the temptation is even more so. Why not try and go for it all—after all, have to be in it to win it, right? Wrong!

This is a very exhausting and time intensive approach, that just doesn't work. (Trust me, been there, done that, got the shirt—not the football shirt which I know nothing about.) We can't be everything to everyone, so it's good to begin by identifying those areas that you can competently write in.

This includes identifying industries and also writing forms. For example: I write business reports, presentations and conduct analysis for IT companies; and I write blog posts for retail companies. (I also have different profiles for each because these are very different industries and styles.) But look into your own background. Did those ballet, tennis, piano lessons teach you anything before you gave them up for other pursuits? Focus, focus, focus—and this will mean that you can quickly build up areas of expertise, rather than coming across as a Jack or Jill or Other of all trades (but expert in none). The cricket columnist at *The Times* doesn't usually comment on 'Today in Parliament'. That doesn't mean the cricket columnist doesn't have an opinion, but an opinion isn't enough.

## A Standout Profile

Before you begin applying for work on a freelancing site, it's important to get your profile right. Potential customers will check your profile to learn about you and what you can offer—get it wrong and it provides the wrong impression, it could mean you end up trying to do work that isn't really your area of expertise, or worse still, you'll disappoint the client, the project won't go well, and everyone ends up disappointed. A rushed profile screams unprofessional and reflects on your work ethics. Take your time and build the right profile—one that reflects the image you want to portray—and you'll attract the right customers.

Freelance platforms can be an effective means to finding freelance work, but just registering an account and throwing together a profile isn't going to achieve results. Listed below are the areas to focus on when building your profile:

> **Top Tip: Have a Coordinated Profile**
>
> If you're serious about having a career as a freelancer, you'll need to put the effort into building an attractive profile. That means thinking about all the components which go into that—it's your job title, your photo and potentially any banner that a freelance platform might let you add. If a travel writer has a banner of a lovely mountain scene, it makes complete sense—if someone who's applying for a gig writing for a food blog a mountain isn't useful… and I'd wonder if they were serious. And on the subject of a photo—take it very seriously. Choose a really good image of yourself (ask friends and colleagues you trust for help) and look the part. As John Berger once said, seeing comes before words.

**Your name/pen name.** Some freelancers don't like to use their own name; others operate under a business name. There are advantages to using your real name—just like in business, it adds a personal touch and can help you stand out—though how will anyone know. So don't pick a pretentious pen name. David John Moore Cornwell is better known as John le Carré and this *nom de plume* suits a British author of espionage novels set during the 1950s and 1960s. But David Cornwell would suit the freelancer better, it's more down to earth. Also, avoid abbreviating your name, for example: John P. or indeed overextending your name to something like Dorothy T. Ward-Sayer, the Third. Simply use a first and last name—as we have done for the cover of this book.

**Decide on your job title/s.** Are you going to promote yourself as a 'Freelance Writer', 'Journalist' or 'Content Marketing Specialist'? These are just a few possibilities (there are so many) but selecting the right title needs careful consideration. You can be a few complementary roles—for example, Content Writer and Editor. And you can also have multiple profiles to reflect the many freelancing 'faces' that you have. Our recommendation is to keep it reasonably generic so as not to limit yourself or deter potential suitable clients.

**Have a headline**. A headline describes your job title. Be specific as possible, to make it easier for your client to understand what you do. Keep it professional and try to focus on specifics to help clients understand your talents—for example, 'eBook Writer' is better than 'Writer'.

**Upload a professional photo**. Selfies and odd close-up photos just don't cut it as a profile photo and can backfire, creating the wrong impression. If you can, get a professional photograph taken or at least dress well and get someone else to take the picture. Keep it close so the focus is on the person not the background. Smiling is essential as it makes you appear more friendly and confident. No sunglasses or photos jumping out of airplanes with a parachute—it's the professional person you should be promoting, not the fun-loving hedonist.

**Your *short* freelancing biography.** This short description summarises what you do and how you do it. Write it in first person to give it that personal edge. Describing yourself in third person can sound like you're narrating a movie. Avoid writing your freelancer profile as if it's a page on a corporate website, or the other extreme, a dating profile. Ideally, your bio should be two to three short paragraphs in length (max. 200 words) and should convey your strengths concisely. Remember, clients will be browsing through lots of profiles, so you need to grab their attention instantly. Try to make it personal but not too personal. Your clients don't need to know how many children (or cats) you have, nor do they need to know your hobbies or football affiliation (which could be a disincentive in any case). The aim is to help someone who doesn't know you very well understand your skills on offer. If you've got some great experience, don't be shy to say so—but there is an art to the 'humble brag', so focus on what you achieved (such as results) and avoid lines such as 'This was the best piece of writing ever'.

**Add your qualifications**. These can go towards the end. Use headings such as 'Employment History', 'Education' and the 'Other Experiences' sections to make it clearer. If you have any writing qualifications—such as a degree in Creative Writing, list it and your university. Not everyone you'll be competing against will have qualifications, so this is another way of helping you to stand out from the crowd.

**Connect your social networks**. Some freelancing platforms allow you to connect your social networks and portfolios with your freelancer profile. Facebook, Twitter, Tumblr, LinkedIn—whatever is incorporated within your personal brand and that you're comfortable sharing with potential clients. Our advice is to have a separate social media platform which keeps your personal life personal. Try to avoid letting your public and personal life collide on social media.

**Add skills**. Freelancing platforms often allow you to select your skills and areas of expertise. Again, try to be specific and focus on your key skills that you will be looking for work in. The more relevant skills you add, the more projects you're likely to match with.

**Skill tests**. 'Take Them If You Can.' The more relevant tests you pass, the more professional you look.

## Making Your Profile Stand Out

- Spell and grammar check: Tools like Grammarly can help check your profile bio for any errors before making it public. This might seem a very obvious point but take a moment and look at some published profiles online—I bet you spot quite a few glaring errors!
- Look at others: If you can't figure out what to write in your description or even how to write it, check out some of the successful freelancer profiles to get an idea. It's also a good lesson in what not to do!
- Ask for reviews: If you do a good job most clients will be happy to leave a review once a job is complete, but you might need to ask.
- Ask for referrals: If your client says you did a great job, ask them nicely to refer you to other clients.
- Add a video: some freelancing platforms allows you to include a video in your freelancer profile. This can help attract more attention to your profile.
- Remember, your freelancer profile is your online CV. So, make it professional and not too personal. Forget about selfies and emojis.
- Keep it up to date! It's all too easy to forget to check up on your profile and it will quickly become dated as you move on, gaining more experience. Put a regular reminder in your calendar to review all your online profiles. That award you won in 2015? It was great back then and you could still list it in 2016—but now it just looks like you're past your 'best by date'!

## The Freelance Writer's Portfolio

A writing portfolio is the best way to show off your skills and achievements professionally. Some freelancing sites require you to have a portfolio of work samples. If not, you can also create your own professional freelancing profile with websites such as https://www.clippings.me/ and https://www.journo-portfolio.com/.

**You, the freelancer**. Your portfolio needs to represent the type of freelance writer you are and the work you want to attract. It's good to show versatility and a range of your skills. It should showcase your *best* work, reflecting your unique style. Your portfolio should definitely *not* contain everything you've ever written. Only include the very best of your recent work (no older than two years). The most effective portfolios are lean, focused and represent the writer's specialty/field.

**Quality not quantity**. When it comes to your portfolio, it's definitely better to focus on quality rather than quality. Depending on where you have your portfolio, usually six to ten pieces are enough. The aim is to give a snapshot of what you can do—not to show them everything you have written since you were ten years old. And it's important that you don't give away anything that might be of value (e.g. we've seen useful templates available on Freelancer's portfolios, which is giving away their valuable content).

**PDFs or JPGs**. Most portfolios are usually a mix of links and PDF or JPEG uploads—don't use Word documents as these can be easily copied. Yes, PDFs can also be copied but it's harder and not everyone has the tools to do this. Links are not ideal as they can be deleted, moved or change over time—so it's better to take a snapshot (copy) of a webpage than to include a link. It can be an option to host the files yourself or set a schedule to come back and check that everything's still where it should be.

**Pay attention to the order of your written work**. Some people display their clippings by date, some prefer to do it by section type—just be consistent. And on the subject of date—don't include examples that are from years past—this only raises the question, what have you been doing in the meantime? Be careful too, a design might date your work (e.g. a webpage from over ten years ago will appear very dated against latest designs and graphics).

**A strong portfolio**:

- shows the versatility of the freelancer's skills and capabilities;
- reflects the freelancer's attention to detail and high standards; and
- demonstrates something of the freelancer's personality.

## Change Your Portfolio Regularly

It's a good tip to compile and maintain a spreadsheet of all your work. Including information such as links to the articles, titles, publication dates, whether the client has given you permission to share the work, and other relevant information for your own personal records. This will enable you to quickly rotate and update your portfolio on a regular basis.

## Refresh Your Content

If your sample work is all from a few years ago, clients will wonder how recent your experience is. And styles date very quickly. When we look at a profile, with a few glances will make assessments—rightly or wrongly—and you want your content to say: my content is fresh and relevant to today! Not, my works from a few years back and I haven't been working ….

## Portfolio Content

The key aspect for content for your portfolio is to keep it professional. You can include pieces that were written as part of say, an academic course. You're not saying that all work in your portfolio were paid commissions, so you can also include work you provided for free for say a friend or volunteer organisation.

### Some Potential Ideas Include

- A recent blog post on a topic you are passionate about
- A piece of writing for a community group, club or university publication
- A press release or other promotional material
- An essay on a controversial topic
- A profile on an interesting person or place
- A short form piece of breaking news
- A feature article
- A research paper
- An editorial
- A personal essay
- Multimedia storytelling
- Collaborative writing of some kind

**Personalise it**. A professional writing portfolio represents you and your personal brand. If you're marketing yourself as a blog content writer, specialising in the wedding industry, you'll want to include your best pieces that show this—ones that reflect your unique voice and ones that are straightforward.

> **Top Tip: PDFs and One-Page Snapshots**
>
> Upload PDFs not Word files. These are harder for people to copy the content from. And you don't need to upload the entire piece. Just the first page is enough—the idea is to provide a taster of what you're capable of, not give your work, and ideas, away. If it's a short story, for example, you don't need to upload the entire piece for someone to ascertain your writing skills (remember, they are assessing your skills, not the short story).

## Volunteering

Writing for free might not seem like a great option, especially when your aim is to make money from your writing. But before you dismiss it too quickly, there are some potential advantages. I volunteered for a childbirth charity when my daughter was a baby—it was a subject that I had a lot to say about at the time and a cause that supported me when I needed it. So, I was happy to give them some of my time. I hadn't really done a lot of professional magazine editing, but they didn't mind, and my graphic design skills very quickly turned their basic magazine into a professional publication. Our membership grew and so did my reputation along with my experience. With thousands of members in my community, it gave me excellent exposure as well as practice, and today I'm the editor of a much larger, nationwide organisation, with international journals which I edit (and it's a paying gig). So, to my mind, it was a worthwhile experience—and I felt good at the time because I gave something back to a good charity.

**Make a difference in your community**. This might seem obvious, but it does actually feel good to actually do something constructive to help a cause you feel strongly about.

**New skills**. One of the best things about non-profit volunteering is the diversity of assignments. Volunteers tend to be versatile because of the organisation's limited budgets, so it's possible you'll get to do things you've not tried before—fantastic for learning on the job.

**New opportunities**: It's very likely you'll get involved in raising public awareness about the issues they represent—and they are always keen to publish articles into the local press.

**Writing practice**: Volunteer writing work is meaningful on a whole different level than paid writing work, and it can help your other writing become more meaningful and authentic.

## How to Have a Positive Volunteering Experience

If you're going to write for a volunteer organisation or charity, you need to make the right choice before you commit. Remember, the people you will be working feel passionately about the organisation or charity, so here are some things to consider:

**Is it an issue you feel passionate about?** This might seem obvious, but it can be easy to lose sight of what's important, especially if presented with something that looks a better option; for example, you may be tempted to choose a flashier, better-known organisation over a lesser known one even though you don't care as much about the issue. Ultimately, you just might enjoy the work much more for a cause you really care about and stick it out for the right reason.

**Start small**. Once you have identified the project for you, don't go in with all guns blazing, offering everything. You just might come to regret that, especially as many such organisations are desperate for help and will grab all offers. Test the waters first with just one assignment. Later, you can increase your hours if you like.

**Treat it like a paying gig**. The volunteer coordinator (or whoever you are reporting to) is the one in charge, and the final decision stops with them. Whether that's decisions or editing your work, its good experience getting use to conforming to requirements of others.

**When you get busy with your paid work, let them know**. Don't feel guilty just let inform them. It's polite and they will understand that you need to make a living too.

**If it's not a good fit, part ways**. Sometimes, volunteer roles just don't work out. Maybe the types of assignments the offer just don't match up with your interests. If you've given it a fair shot, and it's still not working, complete your current assignment and write a polite and professional resignation letter.

**Keep up the communication**: Non-profit managers can get overwhelmed—if weeks go by and you haven't gotten another assignment, be proactive and get in touch.

**Follow their protocol**. Make sure you understand all the privacy rules—and follow them. For example, if you write an article for the organisation's magazine focusing on specific clients, make sure all releases are signed and that you have signed a confidentiality agreement.

**Follow the house style**. It seems obvious to say but everyone wants copy they can just slip into what they are presenting without having to do much to it (mostly because they don't have the time).

# Key Chapter Points

A professional freelancer needs to have:

- A website that represents the person and the services they provide. It needs to be professional, provide details of the freelancer and the services they provide, and demonstrate the quality standards they embody.
- A profile is often the first time a client will encounter us. It seems to catch their attention, be informative and showcase our abilities.
- A portfolio supports our profile. It needs to show just enough to convince a client what we can deliver, but not give any valuable content away.
- Getting experience and sample work is necessary to show clients what were capable of. Volunteering is a good way to not only give us experience, but it also helps to build on our sample work and learn new skills.

**Exercise 6.1**
What are your areas of expertise?

- Brainstorm all the writing forms that you have experience in. You could begin with, blog posts, articles, reviews, interviews and so on.
- Against each one, list again each whether that experience from 1 to 5 (1 being only a little experience; 5 being very experienced). Remove anything that is a 1 or 2.
- Now group them into industries or fields. For example: you might say retail or business or charity. If you don't have much experience in any industry, see if you can group them in some other way. For example, editing or proofreading.
- Hopefully you can now see those fields where your experience lies.

**Exercise 6.2**
Are there any fields you'd like to work in but don't have the experience?

- Brainstorm ideas for gaining experience in these areas.
- Do you know anyone in the field that might give you some work (might be volunteer)? Have a search online for potential charity organisations that might be interested in working with you.
- Could you do some research and write a blog post for your own website, on a relevant subject in this area?
- Is there a forum you could join to build up your knowledge and provide you with useful contacts?

# 7

# Finding Work

In this chapter we will:

1. Explore different sources where you can find work—from the more traditional ways to going online. Work isn't going to come and seek us out, so we need to be proactive and go find it—and that also means being creative with sources.
2. Show and understand how important networks are. Not only will they provide us with contacts and friends in the lonely world of freelancing, but they can also be supportive and provide valuable advice.
3. Come to terms with the fact that customers are for life not just for Christmas (oh hang on … that might be puppy dogs). Anyway, customer relationships are the life blood of our business. We need to nurture them and ensure they grow and foster. We'll discuss how to do this.
4. Get our hands dirty and explore the art of resume/CV writing.

So, you've made the decision to become a freelance writer; you've chosen a business name, designed business cards, setup a website—if you were a business with a premise made out of bricks and mortar, you'd also have the sign ready to go over the door. All you need now is customers to walk over the threshold—or for the freelance writer, for the writing gigs to start rolling in. You might be lucky and have a gig already lined up, but chances are, you'll have to put in hard work, sweat and perhaps tears before you're have writing gigs coming in on a regular basis.

When I first started out it was pretty nerve-racking. There were the ever-frequent worries that my skills might not stack up, compared to other freelancers. And like most freelancers, I was concerned I might go bust within a fortnight because I just didn't charge enough, or the worry that I might be asking too much. Or that clients would take advantage of my naivety and I'd end up earning way less than the minimum wage. But I'm please to say that was over ten years ago and my freelancing work has gone from strength to strength. I've built up customers who regularly get back to me because they like my work, and new ones coming along, often by referral. There has been the rare occasion where I've had my fingers burnt and haven't been able to charge for all the hours I've put it—but on the whole, the vast majority of my clients have been fair and decent to work with. But it hasn't always been easy or plain sailing; we've had to learn some tough lessons along the way, which we'll share with you now, so you can hopefully avoid some of the pitfalls.

Our advice here is to take it slow and steady. Keep your expectations reasonable—don't quit a paying job expecting to live off your freelancing income immediately. It will take time. Start small, if you can, build up your experience and clients when you have other income coming in (I worked nights and weekends when I was starting out). It will take off the pressure and you can test the water before you leap in.

## Finding Work

### Traditional Sources to Find Writing Gigs

**Friends, family, basically anyone you know:** Word of mouth costs nothing and can make a huge difference if you're just starting out and time is more abundant than money. Tell everyone you're looking for work and you just might have a few surprises in store. Somebody who knows somebody, an uncle knows a guy down the pub, an aunt working for a new designer shop, a cousin working for a plumber, roofer, new sports academy—maybe there are such small businesses in your network who could use your writing expertise, you just need to meet. Or they might just know someone who does. It might only be a few hourswork, maybe writing a CV for someone, producing a menu for a restaurant, an advertisement for a hairdresser, a set of flyers for a soccer/ballet/basketball/yoga school—but no job is too small and it's all experience. Do a great job and it might also be a reference and the potential of further work. And the more samples you have to go into your portfolio, the better you're able to convince future clients of your skills.

So, have business cards on you at all times, and be practised in your elevator pitch (we'll get to this in a bit)—so when Miley Cruz comes into the elevator, are you just going to stand frozen to the spot, or are you going to ask if you can write her official biography … and what do you mean you're not a fan? When has that ever had anything to do with it? You're a writer, she might not know she needs a biographer until you offer—even if it's to ghost-write it … hmm, maybe we should do a section on ghost writing. You never know who you might meet, so just be ready to let people know you're available to take on work.

**Cold calling:** Cold calling means what it says on the tin, you're going in cold, contacting someone or a business you've had no prior contact with and you're going to convince them they need your services. It's possible they don't even know they need someone, indeed, do any of us? That's how advertising works—ask yourself how often you've bought something you don't really need but were persuaded to simply by seeing an ad. Or indeed you find out you did need it but up until then didn't know it existed. But before you go cold calling, you need to do your research. Find a business that is genuinely in need of help. Check out their website. Do they advertise in local newspapers? Do they have a strong social media presence? Perhaps it's a dog groomer whose website is woefully out of date (or non-existent!)—if you're a dog person, you could produce a couple of blog posts for them a month—charge them a small sum (do you research online and you'll find the going rate for a post in your location) and it's likely that small investment will pay off well for the business. But small businesses are often tight on funds and can't afford to waste money. Therefore, you need to convince them that your proposition will deliver real value—test the water, do a one off for a very reasonable rate and if they like the results, you just might get a regular piece of work.

Meeting someone in person can make a real difference—if it's possible. Sure, you can email a company and tell them you could provide regular blog content for their outdated website, but chances are your email is just one amongst hundreds. If it's a big company, you don't have much choice. But if it's a small business, say a coffee shop or hairdressers, popping in at a quiet time means you can show them you've made the effort. Better still, get your hair cut there and start up a conversation. Likewise, with the coffee shop, if you're a regular, they're more likely to recognise you and give you some time. They also get the chance to see you and your enthusiasm. So, if it's local, if it's a small business and you can likely speak with the owner (or arrange to), then it's worth giving it a try. Remember, no business is too small—dog groomers, local cafés, hairdressers—these are all small businesses that need customers.

And your writing skills can help them achieve their goals. And with small businesses, one thing which seems to be gaining popularity is 'shared working space'. A bank near me closed down, the building was sold, and 20 startup businesses are now working there. They rent the space, hot desk and so on, and who knows, they might be so busy setting up their business to do the other stuff, like websites and so on ... making sense here? Take a stroll and look out for them, do a search for them in your own town. As I was writing this, I typed 'shared working space' and my location, into Google and was offered 13,000,000 results (0.56 seconds). Okay so the 'results' will be about selling space but then you can see where they are. So, take a stroll down on your way for a mid-day coffee and check them out.

*Timing is key.* Turn up at a café at midday and the owner isn't going to have a minute to spare. But if you arrive at 9.30 in the morning and they only have a customer or two, they may very well hear what you have to say.

*Keep it brief.* How you found out about them. Who you are. What you can do for them (see 'Building Your Elevator Pitch' below).

**Local printers and web design companies.** Printers have local businesses stopping by all the time, and sometimes they have a board or a list of available writers. Likewise, any business that works with clients who also need writers (web design agencies are a good example), it's worth establishing a connection with. They might be happy to add you to their list, or better still, hand out your business card to interested clients. It's worth asking. Remember, it's about forging relationships, so think about what you could offer them. In the future you'll also have clients who might need recommendations of local printers—so ask for their business cards so you can return the favour.

**Local business communities.** Local business owners understand how tough it is to stay in business, and often support each other. You might find local clubs—sometimes they meet up for early morning breakfast or in the evening—so that local business owners can get together and give each other support and advice. I've always found these groups helpful—I once met an IT support business owner—I needed my computer fixing and he needed some writing done for his website. A nice trade and we both went on to recommend each other to various clients.

> **Top Tip: Get Visible**
>
> **Coffee cafés, pubs and so on.** Some of the customers will be small business owners out for a break; ask if you can put cards up, flyers on tables, ads in the window—it's all about visibility.

**Once a client ... always a client.** If a gig has gone well, make sure the client is aware of your full repertoire of skills. A link to your website is a good idea, and a friendly mention that you would be happy to assist them with any future writing needs.

**And don't forget—ask for a reference.** No writing gig is too small to ask for a reference. Once you've landed a few clients and established good working relationships with them, you can consider whether it's a good idea to ask them for a referral. It can be a daunting prospect and they might say no, but they might also appreciate your drive and enthusiasm and say yes. And a few of these on your website look good for other potential customers.

## Online Sources to Find Writing Gigs

**Cold calling, online style.** We talked about cold calling above—but it's an online world, so make the most of it. Get in touch with small businesses that you think might be interested in the services you provide—but put the work in first and do your research, before you send off that email. If they even get a whiff that it is a standard email you send out in bulk, chances are it will go straight into trash. So that means, find out what they do, where you might be able to assist, and find out details so you can personalise your email (such as names). Mention an article on their website and they just might be impressed enough to keep reading. I once came across an online magazine for an upmarket audience. Unfortunately, the articles they were publishing on their blog were littered with typos and grammatical mistakes. Clearly, they weren't proofreading their posts before they went online. I contacted them and told them a few positive things that I liked about their website, but then I ask explained how the poor quality of their posts reflected badly on their brand. It was a wake-up call that, thankfully, they appreciated, and I went on to be their proof-reader.

**Warm pitching.** This approach is far more indirect and is more about building relationships over time. If you find a business in your niche area that you think you could potentially work with, follow them on social media. Over time you might like some of their posts and then you could start engaging in some of their comments. After a while, you might then decide to formally introduce yourself and enquire if there are any writing opportunities. I saw this recently. I was recording and mixing a new record and ended up working with someone who 'warm pitched' his studio. It worked out really well, thank goodness. It would have been hard to say no because we had become friends but actually, I worked with him because I got a chance to see what he did, how he worked and how good his work was.

**Don't neglect your website.** It is all too easy to do. Following all the excitement of setting it up, then comes the more mundane tasks of keeping it fresh and up to date. And, just like the cobbler's children and their woeful shoes, your website will be the first to be ignored if work start coming in. This is a big mistake—clients want to see that you're professional and a high-quality writer—and if your website doesn't reflect this, they'll soon go elsewhere. A good idea is to write a number of 'spare' posts when you have the time, and rather them posting them all in the same week, keep them in reserve for when you're running out of time.

**Don't neglect your social media.** Keep your social media profile up-to-date, and if you're looking for work, advertise that you're available. Sometimes potential clients will think you're busy (that's the impression we want to make!) but a subtle, I'm available for hire, lets them know you can take on work now. And it lets other freelance writers know that you could take on any excess work they might have. And while where on the subject of social media, go easy. It's all too tempting to be on every platform going, but once you have work coming in, you just won't have the time needed to keep them all active. Start with just one or two platforms, and set a regular but achievable schedule—daily would be great, but can you really keep it up? Better to go for once a week and keep those extra posts in reserve.

**Guest blog for another website.** Unless you're a highly sought-after blogger, this will probably be a free writing gig *but* some popular sites have thousands of followers—so that means thousands of people potentially reading your work. That's hugely valuable and could be worth more to you in the long term, that a one-off payment. Building up your reputation won't happen overnight; it's something you need to nurture and grow. And it's possible that one of those readers will remember your work and go on to be a later client. Or maybe even recommend you to someone. So, don't forget your portfolio—if you want to pitch to job advertisements you need to show examples of your work and these don't all need to be from paid commissions.

*Where to guest post?* Do your research—find a site that would be interested in the stuff you like to write—check that they regularly have guest posts and approach them. Even a search on your niche area followed by 'write for us' is worth a try. It's important to check out their guest post guidelines—refer to it in some small way and it will impress them that you've taken the initiative. Finally, have your author bio ready—and always tailor this to the site. What works for one, doesn't necessarily work for others. They don't want your entire history from birth to today—just the relevant bits!

**Investigate freelancing platforms.** These are online marketplaces that bring together freelancers (of all differ types, not just writers) and people, or buyers, who are in need of their services.

We can't vouch for any of these—though we've used various sites from time to time, and the quality of the work can vary greatly for many different reasons. It might be a good period where there are a lot of buyers with interesting projects, or there might be a downturn and there are few decent projects on offer. For example, only four weeks ago there was plenty of work listed, but in recent days, there has been a sudden decline—events happening in the wider world clearly having an impact. As for the work on offer? You need to trust your instinct. If something doesn't sound right or seems a bit suspect, keep looking. Though that sad, there are buyers who have had their fingers burnt as well, so they are also wary. For example, you might find some putting in odd questions at the bottom of their work description—such as state the capital of France at the beginning of your proposal. They do this to test that you do actually read their description, because in all too many instances, the people bidding just haven't bothered to look beyond the job title. Some buyers might ask questions, such as whether you will do the work yourself—this is because some freelancers might outsource it to someone else. It's worth taking a look at what's on offer, but before you commit to anything, always check out their terms and conditions. We'd strongly advise that you start off with the free sites.

Some freelancing platforms to consider:

- PeoplePerHour—freelancing website
- Upwork—procure specialists at reasonable cost
- Twago—online work platform in Europe
- DesignCrowd—freelancing marketplace with project proposals
- Cohort—is all about building up a network and recommendations
- Nexxt—network of skilled and talented professionals
- WriterAccess—find independent writers
- WeWorkRemotely—companies post only jobs that can be done remotely
- Envato—find an expert to collaborate with on a particular project
- Fiverr—a global online marketplace that has millions of freelancers around the world
- Guru—discover freelance workers for commissioned work
- Elance—online staffing portal that connects employers to employees
- Freelancer.com—freelancing, outsourcing, and crowdsourcing marketplace

**Try a job board.** If you're just starting out and wanting to land a few jobs without finding them yourself, responding to a job ad on a job board, can be a good choice. And it's not just new writers that turn to job boards. Many writers use it for finding consistent work—it might not pay as much, but at the beginning, getting regular work coming in is all important. Not just that, it's a huge confidence boost when you land your first writing gig. An advantage to using job boards over a freelance marketplace (like PeoplePerHour or Upwork) is that there is no bidding. Anybody can post a job advertisement—entrepreneurs, small businesses, startups, individuals—and you pitch to these ads. The job ad might specify a rate, or otherwise you provide your rate.

While there are paid job boards you can use, if you just want to try it out, stick with the free job boards. Some job boards to start pitching to: Problogger, Blogging Pro, All Freelance Writing Job Board, Contena. These job boards also have a social media presence, so it can be worthwhile keeping an eye on their posts as it can a useful signpost to quickly finding potential writing gigs.

**Check out LinkedIn and other job sites.** LinkedIn also have a job board, so it's worth trying your niche and 'writer' and seeing what comes up. And it's worth searching through other general job sites such as Indeed and Monster.

**Try online magazines.** This isn't the easiest work to land, and it will take time, but there are plenty of online magazines paying for contributions, so it's worth doing your research. It's key to get the match right—find the publications that have previously published work similar to yours.

**Work for content agencies.** These are businesses that act as a middleman between businesses that want writers and the freelancer. The smaller agencies (such as Word Candy) tend to pay better and sometimes they offer training and support. You won't earn as much as you would finding the gigs yourself, but it's a way to get started and can provide some regular work.

**Pitch, pitch, pitch.** For many print journalists and writers, when they decide to go online and freelance, they focus on writing for publications and selling their stories. It's good work if you can get it, but it's very inconsistent and there is loads of competition. But that's not to say it isn't worth giving it a try—remember that portfolio of samples you're trying to build up?

To find this type of work it's all about going online and researching. Publications have websites which will tell you how to submit your ideas. Typically, your cold pitch your idea first and if they like it, you're away.

**Write for free.** What?!??!? We hear you exclaim. Have we gone mad? Surely this book is about making a living and how are we going to do that if we give away your talents for free. But, stay with us, there can be instances where it is definitely worthwhile.

While you might be writing for free, it does bring other benefits:

- Gives you experience that can go into your CV.
- Provides you with samples to show potential clients. Samples are important, especially if responding to Job Ads. It's all good and well to tell the potential client how great a writer you are, but they want to see it for themselves. No samples, and it's going to be a tough job landing it.
- Will hopefully result in testimonials.
- Boosts your confident.
- Potentially result in additional (paid) work.

> **Top Tip: Set Boundaries If You're Writing for Free**
>
> Make it clear with the client what it is exactly you are providing for free. For example, it might be one blog post of 200 words. Explain upfront that you're investing your time to show them what you could provide. Just manage expectations, and if they want more, that's great. Just explain this upfront.

## Engaging in Networks

Some new freelancers are reluctant to network with other freelancers, fearing they are competition. This is a big mistake. Being in contact with other writers, and building up a network, can be hugely beneficial. Not only are they in a similar situation to you, but they can offer advice and sometimes work. I had to get a slow puncture on a car tyre repaired. It was fairly urgent; I had a long trip coming up. The guy I called couldn't come and do it, but he gave me the number of somebody else, a competitor as it turned out and said, 'he's a good guy, does good work.' After the tyre was fixed I told him the story and he said, 'Yeah, we do each other favours all the time, there's a couple of us, it balances out and the customers appreciate it.' Don't be shy sharing your hourly rate with other freelance writers either—that way you can all ensure that you are charging within a typical market range. The tyre guys all charged roughly the same. If you're charging more, that's okay, maybe your skills warrant it—but it's good to know, in case other clients are reluctant to pay the same. If you're charging a lot less than the market average, consider revising your rates. Being at the bottom end of what other freelancers charge can create the impression that you're cheap for a reason—not as good—and that's not what you want. If you've made a strategic decision to charge less in a bid to attract more business, give it a try—but not for too long, or you'll just work too many hours for too little pay. That's not a good situation for anyone to be in.

Having a second opinion on quoting the number of hours for a particular piece of work, can be invaluable. Just remember it's give as well as take. I keep up regular contact with numerous other freelance writers—some local to me so we can meet up and have coffee—but others are online friends that I've never met in person. They also referred work to me when they've been busy, and I've returned the favour on numerous occasions.

There are other networks you can also consider:

- Local business communities
- Other freelancers (such as graphic designers, website builders etc.)
- Online communities
- Niche industries

## Building Customer Relationships

Regardless of whether you meet your clients in person, or they remain remote, establishing and maintaining a good working relationship is key to any successful business.

**Agree job requirements before you start.** In your eagerness to get started and deliver, it can be tempting to just get going—don't! If you don't meet the buyer's expectations, you'll spent a lot more time (that you can't charge for) and potentially disappoint everyone involved. Before you begin, agree their expectations and document the job requirements—doesn't need to be a fancy document. A bullet pointed email is fine—and ask them to confirm they agree. Then you can start.

**Keep up the communication.** Clients like regular updates on progress. If something comes up and you need to change something that was agreed upfront—immediately contact the client, explaining the situation and the options available. If the client contacts you, it's manners to respond within 12 hours—even if it's just to say you'll need to investigate and get back to them within 24 hours.

**Commit to any deadlines.** Your client has a business and may be depending on your work. If something genuinely comes up then you can discuss it with your client, but unless it's extremely important, keeping to your deadlines impresses the client and keeps them happy.

**Commit to word counts.** Your client might be precise about space, precision and content. Just because a little purple prose opens up the poetic possibilities and you are beginning to enjoy the cascade of words burbling up a pebble beach, just as the night sky turns pink as the sun sets, while the moon smiles down on a benign world, it doesn't mean it's of any use to anyone written down. Get the right words in the right order and don't stop to take in the view.

**Changes will happen.** You've started the project and discovered things are very different that you'd expected. They love your work, and in addition to that post they'd like you to take a quick look at an article and proofread it. That's okay—you want to keep the client happy—but don't say yes to everything without considering the impact. If the customer increases the work brief, document it and if it increases the amount of work, make this clear. It's then their choice if they want to proceed with spending the extra amount.

> **Top Tip: Don't Jeopardise Quality**
> 
> It's important to deliver a quality result, so don't cut corners when it comes to editing and proofreading. Always allow enough time for these important tasks. Submit work that is sub-standard, and you'll soon regret it.

**Try to keep your client happy.** The last thing you want is the customer requesting a refund or cancellation. Even worse is complaining—and let's face it, complaining online draws attention and doesn't go away. It can impact your rating and hinder your opportunities for future work. Sometimes it better to write something off as a lesson learned and move on. What's important is that you avoid it happening again. If extra work was due to poor communication or a poorly defined brief upfront, then you can avoid this next time. It's generally better to maintain the client relationship and swallow your pride; you can always decide to not work with them again, but it's better not to end it on a bitter note. Bad word of mouth is not what you want.

**Raise an invoice when the job is done.** You can request the payment, including the release of funds held in a holding account, when the task is completed. With some of the freelancing sites, if you communicate outside of the system, they won't assist you if things get difficult with the customer and you can be suspended. Be professional and create a standard template for your invoices including your business logo and set a timescale for payment which you can work with—14 days, three weeks, it's up to you. In our experience, people tend to respect your deadlines because they have their own expectations of customers, but they are equally happy to let it slide if you don't specify.

# Creating a Freelancer's CV

> Simple can be harder than complex: You have to work hard to get your thinking clean to make it simple. But it's worth it in the end because once you get there, you can move mountains. Steve Jobs (Apple)

You might have a CV/resume already and this is a good starting point for building your freelancing CV. But it's important to remember that a freelancer CV is rather different to a standard CV. The key difference is that a freelancer tends to have a lot more short-term experience to include verses someone who has been an employee. A freelance doesn't just work at a series of jobs; they are building up their own business working for a range of clients—and a busy freelance might have well over 50 clients in a year—they probably can't even fit all their gigs on onto one page.

Your CV is never going to represent who you are, especially as a freelancer—because as freelancer is a chameleon. I have numerous versions of my CV to reflect the different fields of expertise I have. For example, my IT clients are not interested in my work writing articles for travel magazines, nor vice versa. So, I have one version that's focused on my IT experience and another on my travel.

> **Top Tip: Keep Your CV to Two Pages (Three at the Most!)**
> Here comes the tough part for an experienced freelancer—try to keep it to two pages (three at the most). And I focus on the recent stuff. Any more than ten years ago and they're really not interested.

Don't forget to include all your social media and website details—you can be sure they will check you out online, so make sure your online presence is professional!

We hope you won't do this but it's a very important point, so well make it—be honest and don't stretch the truth. If you're hired based on something you've said in a CV or profile and they discover it's no true, then it's reflects very badly on your professionalism.

Finally, you're a writer so any potential clients will be unforgiving if they find a typo or grammatical error in your CV. So, proofread and proofread again. And again, just to be sure.

## CV Style

A traditional CV will list the person's jobs chronologically but for a freelancer who works many short-term gigs, this could mean that your most relevant experience—while only a short while ago time wise—could end up some way down the list.

Therefore, you can go one of two ways:

- Organise by chronology: Your experience appears as one item sorted by date.
- Organise by skill/expertise and then chronology: List four to six of your focus skills and then sort projects/titles by date for each skill. This option works well of you want to focus on particular skills as these can go at the top.

Should you go all out and make it look fancy? There are two camps on this one—the recruitment industry like to see CVs that are professional and simple. They prefer a simple Word document that can be copied into their own format. No fancy fonts, formatting or layouts. However, you're a freelancer, so much less likely to be dealing with recruiters. And you're a creative artist—therefore, we personally think letting some of your creative abilities shine through isn't a bad thing—and can actually help you standout. Take a look at www.canva.com. They have loads of free templates that you can tailor your CV. Just keep it attractive and don't go over the top. You want to standout for all the right reasons. I tend to have my CV in both formats—that way if a recruiter asks for a simple version, I can send it to them straight away. BUT I have been told that some recruiters rely on scanning software, so it's possible a PDF resume might be overlooked. Best advice is to have both and take into consideration if you're sending it direct to a person, or to a generic email address.

## Profile

Always begin your CV with a profile. This is a brief statement (five to eight lines, no more!) covering who you are and what you do. It's where you make it clear what you offer to the client. Don't focus on describing yourself but describing what you can do for your potential client. They're just not that interested in you—what they really want to know is how you can help them! Think of your skills and then example the benefit: I have strong time management skills, which results in my agreed project deadline's always being met.

## Skills List

Break your skills/expertise areas down into a manageable list—if a client is looking for certain skills—make sure they're on the top of this list. You've probably got loads of skills you could list—but don't be tempted—the potential client will just get lost and not see the ones they're interested in. Focus on the ones that client is looking for. Limit your skills list to just words: For example: blogs, articles, features, reports. Bullet points are good because they stand out.

## CV Highlights

Once you start building up experience, it's important to help potential clients see your relevant work. This is where highlighting can help. This allows you to put 'spotlights' on the gigs you most want them to know about. A potential client doesn't want to know everything you've done—just what's relevant to them! It's better to list a few relevant gigs then a load of ones that have nothing in common with what they do.

A highlight is a brief description of a piece of work, or writing gig, that really stood out and was impressive! Keep it brief—but sell yourself. Don't go over the top and exaggerate. It's all too easy to look things up online (such as LinkedIn), so don't say you were the Project Manager if you weren't. A potential client can potentially find out, and that's it; all trust is lost. Focus on what the problem was—for example, perhaps there was low traffic to the website, and then what you did on the project—for example, researched potential topics and wrote relevant articles. And finally, what the outcome was—hopefully an increase in traffic (and state numbers—that always impresses).

Tailoring our CV:

- Constantly record your gigs with a short description of each. Once you've been freelancing for a while, it becomes difficult to remember everything you've done.
- Keep a spreadsheet that you can quickly refer back to.
- Whenever you're applying for a piece of work, select the projects that are most relevant to the gig you're applying for.
- Keep it brief: two to three lines per highlight should be enough.
- Don't be shy: if you've done some great work, say so! If clients have given you permission to name them, then do so. If it's a recognisable company, all the better, but if not, given a brief description of who they are and what they do.
- Job title: you're a freelancer so you can be inventive—just keep it relevant.
- Remember to be a 'do-er' and use verbs to begin each description.
- Include testimonials, if you can.

## Other Sections

- Contact details—make sure these are easy to find—email address and contact number is sufficient. They don't need to know your home address.
- Qualifications—If you have university qualifications state the university where you graduated from. Once you have your degree, you don't need to state your school grades.
- Any relevant training—again, needs to be relevant.
- Language skills—always useful, but list if you are fluent, competent or basic.
- Hobbies/Interests—only if relevant (if you're applying for a gig to write about scuba diving and it's something you're experienced at—definitely show it). Otherwise, don't tell them you like to travel, bake cakes or own ten cats (unless you're applying to a cat charity!)—keep it relevant!

## Building Your Elevator Pitch

An elevator pitch is an overview of your business, and you should be able to deliver it in the time it takes to complete your average elevator ride (about 30 seconds or less). The aim is to be short and snappy to entice your would-be prospect to want to know more about you and your business. Another way to think about this is as your LinkedIn headline or your Twitter bio. It's basically who you are and what you want in a freelance career.

The elevator pitch goes beyond simply relaying what it is you do. Instead, you want to intrigue your listener so that they want to know more. So, instead of saying, 'I'm a content writer', you might say, 'I help busy small business owners produce content that attracts more customers.' Any small business owners who heard that would likely want to know how they could earn more by doing less.

Have a hook! We're writers so we know what a good hook does—it grabs attention. Your hook could be a simple question, 'So many small business owners waste time and money because they wear too many hats—I'm a freelance content writer that can free up those businesses to focus on what they do best—while I can deliver what I do best—writing outstanding copy.'

Practise your elevator pitch and speak it out loud. It needs to sound natural otherwise it feels too much like a sales pitch. Become comfortable with your pitch, such that when the opportunity arises, it will flow like it's a natural part of the conversation. Just like your business cards, an elevator pitch is a quick way to not just introduce your business to people you meet, but to create interest. Which can hopefully lead to work.

## Key Chapter Points

- Writing gigs can be found in many and varied places. We need to keep our eyes open and our elevator pitches ready. We need to tell everyone and anyone what we do and that we're open for business. This isn't the time to be a shrinking violet. It's a time to be positive, engaging and brief. Don't bore the pants off people with a long speech—short and snappy, leaving them thinking, wow! This person knows their stuff.
- Networks provide the Freelancer with support and advice. It can be a sounding board when you need another opinion, or it might even be the opportunity for work. But it needs give as well as take, so if you want others to help you, you need to also be prepared to help them.
- We want our customers to recommend us to others and keep coming back. So, this means putting in the time to establish good working relationships. It's not about a one-off opportunity. It's investing in a relationship that will grow over time and hopefully result in further opportunities. If you have this mindset from the state, hopefully so will they.
- Freelancers *must* have a CV. They will probably have many. Make it look attractive. Make it stand out.

**Exercise 7.1**
Build your elevator pitch:

1. Start with who you are—one sentence that describes what it is you do. For example, 'I'm a writer who produces content for small business owners.'
2. What services do you offer—keep it brief, one or two sentences is fine—but sum up the type of services you provide. Perhaps it's regular blog posts, or website content, or articles on a particular niche subject.
3. What problem do you solve—identify the value you can bring to a potential customer. Perhaps you can provide regular content. Take a look at their website and if it hasn't been updated in some time tell them you could make it better; provided your services are affordable, they just might be interested.
4. Ask a question—find out what their biggest pain point is. Why isn't hasn't their blog had a post for months? Perhaps work has picked up for them and they no longer have the time. A freelance like you could be just the solution to keeping their web profile fresh and up to date.
5. Why you?—what sets you apart from other freelancers? Perhaps you are local, have a particular interest in the subject matter, and have expertise in the industry? Convince them you're the right person.

# 8

# Navigating the Bid Process on Freelancing Platforms

In this chapter we will:

1. Explore how to identify suitable work opportunities from the sometimes mountains of jobs listed.
2. Discuss how to write a successful bid.
3. Look at proposals and how to write these.
4. Consider how to get your proposal noticed.
5. Reflect on the importance of following-up and getting references.

## Freelancing Platforms: How Do They Work?

Freelancing platforms are effectively job boards for short-term projects. We listed some potential ones to have a look at in Chap. 7.

A client posts work requirements and freelancers find jobs; it's as simple as that. These 'jobs' or 'projects', might be as brief as a few hours' work, and others are for an ongoing, long-term commitment. These sites are often for all freelancers—be that artists, writers, designers and so on, but it's good to view them because you get a feel for the wider business of freelancing (and besides you might be developing side talents of your own—have you done a course on Photoshop lately, for example?). Who is who, though?

**Buyers** are potential clients who post projects on the freelancing platform looking for someone to service a need. They simply post details of their project along with a description of what they require. Typically, there is no one checking these, so it's a real mixed bag when it comes to quality. Buyers can also look through profiles, portfolios and feedback to sellers when they bid on a project. And they can also invite individual sellers to bid on a project.

**Sellers** are freelancers, like you, who can bid for the available projects. They are effectively, selling their services. They may also post offers and promote their wares. These are usually defined services such as editing or proofreading, and they charge a fixed fee. Sellers create a profile page with a headshot and background cover. They include a description of their services, sometimes there is the option to select skills from a list, and they'll list an hourly rate. They can also upload a portfolio of their work that buyers will be able to see.

**How do freelancing platforms make their money**? It's very simple, they link companies or individuals with freelance work needs (buyers) with suitable freelance contractors (sellers), and they get a percentage from the deal.

## Identifying Suitable Opportunities

When freelancers first go onto a freelancing platform, it's often a bit like letting a child lose in a sweet shop. They see all this work on offer, and they're convinced they could probably do a lot of it. And it's tempting to apply to many of the projects on offer, in the hope that the more you send off, the better chance you have of getting something, right? Wrong. Let's stop there. First and foremost, you need to be very clever with your searching. I have learnt from experience; the scattergun approach can be a real time waster and no freelancer has endless time to waste.

Clever searching tips:

- Be specific. For example, rather than just writer be more specific: grant writer, contract writer, article writer. If you can identify a particular field.
- Don't limit yourself to standard terms. The buyers might not always use these—for example, they might title it 'Blog writing' rather than 'Content writing'. Try article rather than writing or content.
- Read the project description—that might sound a bit obvious, but you will be surprised at the number of buyers who place a trick question at the end of their description (e.g. name the capital of France at the beginning of your proposal) just to test that you did actually read it to the end. In an attempt to land work, some freelancers go only by the title and send of a standard generic proposal. This is a very big waste of time.
- Look for projects that have a good match to your skills. If it's a very vague description, then a lot of people will apply and it's difficult to know what

exactly they're looking for. This is one I just came across: *Need a serious writer that can write serious stories! Ten pages! Can be lots of different subjects!* This doesn't really tell us anything—and pretty much anyone who can creatively write could apply. And what's a serious story? That's really open to interpretation.

Things to look for:

- See if other sellers (freelancers) have asked questions from the buyer. This can be a useful way to find out more, and you can also avoid asking the same questions again (which can be annoying and time wasting for the buyer). And sellers questions can often provide you with other useful information—and potentially something you might want to avoid. It's also a way of seeing if anyone has thought of something you haven't—always useful, none of us know everything.
- Look at the buyer's history. Are they new to the platform? Or have they completed a number of projects? Just because they haven't used the platform before, it doesn't mean you should avoid them, but if they're experienced, you have an indication that other freelancers have found them okay to work with.

If a project description is poorly written, should you walk away?

First impressions can sometimes be to move on, but my experience has been that these can be sellers who simply do not have English as a first language—and they want help. Just because a buyer isn't able to draft a great project description, don't dismiss them too quickly. It's very possible it's a good opportunity for someone who is good at writing and communication. Trust your instinct here, this is probably someone putting a call out for help because he/she/they really need it.

This is a project I found earlier, and it made me smile:

Hi—I need an English Academic Writer. You must knowledge about this topic.

I need 2 content 1 is 550 word another is 1000 word. I sent my guidelines after cheek your previous job. Thank You.

But that said, there is a lot of work in tidying up assignments to be written in English when English isn't a first language (which is how this reads).

What if it's very brief?

Personally, I wouldn't waste too much time on it. You just don't know what they're looking for so it's like trying to aim for a target blindfolded. Your chances of hitting the bullseye are slim.

What about the price the buyer is willing to pay? How important is this?

This gives you an indication of what they are prepared to pay—but that doesn't mean they don't have a little in reserve if they come across a great candidate that they think is perfect for the role. Do your maths and work out how much you'd earn per hour given how long you think it would take you to complete the task. If it's way too low, then move on. If it's just a bit too low, you can always put in your proposal, and tell them your rate. But ultimately, if you want or need the job it can be good for your CV—especially at the start.

> **Top Tip: Trust Your Instinct**
>
> You'll find all sorts of projects on freelancing platforms. And some of them will be dodgy (and there is no better word to describe them). They might be dodgy in lots of different ways—it might be the intentions for the work; it might be something other than is being described. The buyer could be fraudulent. My best advice is to trust your instinct. If something doesn't feel right about a project, at any stage in the bid process, walk away. And if you discover something isn't right, let the platform know so that other freelancers don't get caught in future.

## Writing Successful Bid Responses/Proposals

A proposal is a statement to convince someone that you are the right person for a project or piece of work. When you place a bid on a piece of work, you enter a highly competitive process, competing against other freelancers with similar skills. Unless you make your strengths and experience shine in your proposal, you're unlikely to make the shortlist.

### Read the Project Description: And Then Read It Again

It's important to fully understand what is required and what the buyer is looking for. Then you can decide if you're a good match. If you're not a great match—but figure you could do it—still don't waste your time. There will be freelancers who are a better match. It's a better use of time to focus on those opportunities that you have a reason change of success.

This is one I found earlier:

> *We are launching a new wellness e-commerce site specialising in men's and women's wellness products. We are looking for an eclectic mix of content writers and bloggers to create new content for our site on a regular basis. Topics; Men's health and mental health, sleep wellness, wellness technology, wellness trends.*

I have written articles on health and wellbeing previously, so I'm a reasonable match for this one. And I have a few ideas for other topics. The buyer has provided a reason indication of what the work entails—with a few topics listed already. And it also says it's on a regular basis. So, I am getting reasonably good vibes about this one.

## Make an Impression

The top two lines of your proposal sell you and your talents. When the person receives your proposal, these are the lines that will make her/him decide to keep reading or move on to the next bid. If they required something specific—perhaps experience in a particular area—put it near the top. They be looking for it and if they don't find it quickly, it's likely they won't read the rest of your proposal.

This is a pretty common opening line that I've seen in loads of proposals:

*I am a professional copy writer with experience producing website copy for a number of retail companies…*

What's wrong with this? It's fair to say that buyers are a pretty ego-centric bunch. It's all I, I, I, with them! They really don't care if you've written speeches for the Dalai Lama or won the UN Prize for Peace, they only want to know if you can deliver what they are after.

If I was going to apply for my e-commerce role above, I'd try something like:

*With four years' experience writing articles on health and wellbeing websites, I have the skills and knowledge to deliver the e-commerce blog posts you're after.*

I've managed to both sell my skills while acknowledging what they're looking for. It's a good start.

## Sell Your Specific Strengths

What is your most marketable trait? Include it underneath any required responses. This trait may vary depending on the project. For example, if you are applying for a job that is academic, your degree will be the first thing you highlight. On the other hand, if the job requires a specific skill set, you want to focus on your experience. On rare occasions, such as when the employer needs a job finished within 24-hours, you can put something such as a time estimate near the top.

Like my e-commerce role above, I'm also experienced in writing for a range of other websites including IT and Technology businesses, but as these skills aren't relevant to the role, I just don't mention them.

Again, remember those buyers really don't care what you're good at—it needs to be relevant to what they want!

## Details of Your Proposal

This is the body of your response. These aren't job applications, so unless they have asked for a lot of details, you should be able to keep it to half a page, one page maximum. Any more and they will just move on. Lengthy proposals can be daunting—especially if it's just a small piece of work.

Make it personalised for the work advertised. It is fine to have some standard responses up your sleeve but it's pretty obvious when it's a standard response and the seller has taken no effort to personalise it. A buyer will have a lot of potential candidates to choose from—so don't give them reasons to reject you before they're even read beyond your first paragraph.

Refer to points they raise in their project description. If they specifically say they want native English speakers, explain that you are. It might seem obvious to you, but if they're asking, it's important to them.

Remember my e-commerce project: *In the body of my proposal for my e-commerce project, I would refer to specific blog posts I have written on topics related to the ones they have listed.*

## Personalise Your Bid

It takes more time, but a generic bid screams 'I just couldn't be bother' to a buyer. If you respond with a tailored proposal, demonstrating that you've considered all of their requirements and asking any pertinent questions, it will show your experience as well as focus on providing good customer service.

Here's a personalised response to a bid for a charity that helps young people find homes, based in Bondi Sydney (Australia), looking for a blog article writer:

> *Dear Mary,*
> *I am writing to you regarding your proposal searching for a blog article writer. I am a professional writer with my own blog have written guest posts for other blogs. I*

have written for other charities before, including the RSPCA. This is their website and I have included this post in my portfolio.

I grew up in Bondi and have a fondness for the southern suburbs of Sydney, that naturally draws me to your cause. Additionally, as a young adult myself, I relate very much to the struggle of becoming a homeowner in the present time. These experiences and my writing ability encourage me to believe that I would be suitable for your cause. I look forward to hearing from you.

Yours faithfully,
Sara

## Answer Any Questions

Next, be sure you answer any questions the employer might have asked. Sometimes these questions can be answered throughout your text (even at the top); other times you can just set them in their own paragraph. Just make it clear and obvious that you're responding to their questions. They might say they are looking for someone who is good at delivering to deadlines—explain why you are—and that you're committed to your clients.

## Provide Estimates

After you have explained why you would be the best person to complete the project, then it is time to provide time and cost estimates. Sometimes it's just not possible to provide an estimate. In my e-commerce example, the buyer hasn't stated how long they want the posts to be, or how many they want. What I can do, is provide an estimate, for example: I can produce a blog post of between 500–750 words, for £/$ xx. I would then ask questions, such as how many posts they want, and the typical length. In addition, I would ask if they will be provided information to go into the posts or if I will be doing the required research. And if that's part of the role, then I'd charge an amount for this.

If it's too vague, ask questions and explain why you are unable to give a specific quote. Most buyers do not like placeholder bids, so ask questions before bidding.

## Be Polite

Finally, thank the buyer for reading your proposal. Make an impression, so that even if you are not chosen for that particular project, they might think of you for future projects. If you are awarded the project, you will be starting off on the right foot! We all want to work with people who are easy to get along with, trustworthy, and actually fun at times.

## Supporting Your Proposal

Winning proposals are backed by strong profiles and portfolios, and winning profiles alone can get you jobs. Attach work samples or point them to your portfolio with relevant samples of your previous project uploaded.

> **Top Tip: Get in Early**
>
> Buyers will often review proposals in the order they arrive, so you'll increase your chances if you get in early. Some projects attract a lot of interest, especially if left on a freelancing profile for a few weeks, so get your response in as soon as you see it, and you'll be towards the top of the post.

## The Price

This is a guide but isn't set in stone. Sometimes there is room for flexibility, especially if a seller is offering exactly what they are after. It's about providing value for money, so keep it reasonable. If you're new to freelancing, it can be tempting to go in with a lower price to secure the work. This is okay initially as it helps build up your portfolio, but it's not a long-term strategy and you'll quickly burn out. As your experience grows, ensure your price reflects your skills and expertise.

## Your Questions

Questions show that you have read the project description and given it some thought. You might have a question about the work required, durations, if it's an on-off or the potential for ongoing work. It also shows that you've given thought to their project and care about making it a success. Too many freelancers send out generic responses which reflects they not really interested and just want the gig.

## Show Your Experience

A buyer is keen to see that you've done similar work in the past, so providing samples will strongly enhance your bid. This could be through URLs, or uploaded screenshots or files, but ensure you have permission if it is work delivered for another customer.

## Be Clear with What You Will Provide

Especially when it comes to providing writing, editing and proofreading services. If you don't state up-front—you might find yourself spending a lot of hours sending the copy back and forth as the buyer continues to make changes.

Here's an example of a short bid that both asks more details and details what will be included in the service:

> *Dear Jeremy*
> *As a Professional Writer with three years' experience in both editing and proofreading, I feel I am a good fit for the project you have described. I have also worked as a copyeditor for the literary magazine, LET'S WRITE. Further, I understand that the role requires transcription and understand formatting conventions, of which I am particularly strong in.*
>
> *For a 30-page document, I would need to see a short excerpt to enable me to give a definitive fixed price and time estimate, as this will be down to the amount of editing that will need to be done. Is your document clean or full verbatim?*
>
> *If you choose to continue with project with me, you will receive the following:*
>
> - *one document with my edits*
> - *one round of revisions with MS track changes*
> - *one document of the final product, with comments deleted*
> - *Thank you for taking the time to review my application.*
>
> *I hope to have the opportunity to discuss this project with you further.*
> *Kind regards,*
> *Matt*

## Manage Expectations

It's tempting to make grand promises in the hope of winning the work. But securing the bid is only part of the process. If you're unable to deliver to expectations, it will do more harm than good—poor reviews and complaints reflect badly on the freelancer.

## Proposal Outline

Depending on the size of the project, you may not need all of the following sections, but it gives you an outline of what can be included:

| | |
|---|---|
| Proposal title | Give it a title |
| Proposal date | This is the date that you are responding |
| Purpose | Why are you writing? (1 sentence) |
| | For example, *to propose a solution to the problem of… I have identified an opportunity to expand…* |
| Background information | Any details that will help the reader better understand what you are proposing. (50–100 words) |
| | If proposing a solution, briefly outline the problem it will solve. |
| Objectives | What will your idea achieve? Why would your reader want it? (50–100 words) |
| | Will it support an objective? |
| | If proposing a new idea, what opportunity will it provide? |
| | **If it's a small piece of work, then it's possible you don't know, when writing your bid response, what the objectives are—that's okay. |
| Solution/idea description | Succinctly describe the idea that you are proposing. (200–500 words) |
| Cost breakdown | This could be in regard to time and effort, and materials. |
| Any proposed timing | A proposal is early stages so it can only be a rough outline at this stage, for example, four to six weeks. It's also possible that you might only include the timing for next steps. For example, you might need to conduct research to build a comprehensive plan. |
| Proposed team | Might be actual names or simply role titles, but if you need particular people for a project, say they as soon as it is known because getting them available might not be easy. |
| Why this team | Any relevant experience/past projects that were similar? (50 words) |
| Next steps | If this proceeds, what are the next actions? |
| Any questions | State any relevant questions that might be pertinent to the idea. (50–100 words) |
| | Researching the proposal might have uncovered something pertinent. |
| Conclusion | Quick summary of problem and proposed solution, or opportunity and idea. (50–100 words) |

## Getting Your Proposal Noticed

- If the buyer provides their name, use it! Dear Andy, immediately starts off on the right foot, rather than 'Dear Sir' or 'Whom it may concern'. Take their lead—if they address you by Dear Sir/Madam, then do the same.

- Be polite. It might seem obvious, but it can help make you stand out for the right reasons, as well as helping create the impression that you'll be easy to work with.
- Nobody likes to be told they're wrong. It's much better to gently suggest options and let them consider them—they will then think they are their own conclusions and more committed. Of course, you suggested it, but swallow your pride and let them take the credit.
- Have some of your personality shine through. Professional doesn't mean dry or sounding like it's been written by a computer. It helps to build rapport and trust.
- Try to match the tone of the job description. If it's more formal—reflect this. Likewise, if it's more laidback and casual, try to be like this as well. Don't overdo it but you can relax a little.
- Be specific and give examples. Don't just say you have e-commerce experience. Say who it was for, when you did it, and if possible, give them a link to see the post you wrote.
- Be enthusiastic but in a contained manner. Sometimes we can take it too far, and it becomes a bit too sugary sweet.

## You've Won the Bid: Now What?

**Agree clear job requirements before commencing work**. You can only meet the buyer's expectations if you receive a clear brief. If it's just a small piece of work, this brief might only be an email—but it provides clarification and agreement that this is what the buyer wants. This is the document you will come back to if there are disagreements in the future and the buyer is unhappy with what you have delivered, so make sure all the job requirements are provided by the buyer before you begin work.

**Provide regular updates**. Even if the buyer doesn't ask for them, you should provide regular progress updates and record any changes to the brief. It's good etiquette to response to your customer's queries within one working day.

**Commit to any deadlines agree with the buyer**. The buyer has other commitments and a business to run, so they are dependent on you delivering to your commitments. While things can come up which can potentially throw all our plans into chaos, it's important to build contingency into your plans to allow for this. If you think something will take you five days—don't commit to five days! Tell the buyer it will take you six days, and then you have a day spare. All goes well, and you'll impress them by coming in a day early.

**Document any changes**. If the buyer increases the work brief, document this and if it increases the amount of work, make this clear. Being obliging and willing is good, but you need to remember this is business, and if the project brief increases, then the buyer needs to agree to this and to the additional expenditure. They can always change their mind.

**Avoid an unhappy buyer**. Try to avoid the customer requesting a refund or cancellation. This can impact your rating and hinder your opportunities for future work. So, try to find a workable solution.

**Raise an invoice when the Job is done**. You can request the payment, including the release of funds held in the Escrow Account when the task is completed. The buyer must pay your invoice within seven days (or as agreed). Another top tip, though—chase up invoices and remind people where necessary; it's usually the last thing on their mind, but they are used to chasing their own bills so they will understand.

With some of the freelancing sites, if you communicate outside of the system, they won't assist you if things get difficult with the customer and you can be suspended.

## Key Chapter Points

- On freelancing platforms, buyers post project descriptions that they are looking for sellers (or freelancers) to bid on. Sellers create profiles and portfolios that promote their skills and abilities.
- It can be tempting to apply for any project that you think you could do. This can be an extremely time heavy strategy, with poor returns. Better to search other projects that have a strong match to your skills and experience.
- Read through the project description—if a project isn't a good match, move on.
- Tailor, tailor, tailor. Plenty of sellers will send of generic responses to everything and anything. This means that buyers have a lot of poor-quality bids to trawl through. Therefore, you can stand out by taking the effort to tailor your response, demonstrating to the buyer that you've read their project description.
- Ensure you update your portfolio to include work samples that support your proposal.
- Finally, buyers want to work with real people that they hope they will get along with. So, don't be afraid to let your personality shine through.

**Exercise 8.1**
Go onto a freelancing platform such as PeoplePerHour and find a role you're interested in.

Note down the following:

- Make a list of the key skills the buyer is looking for.
- What skills and previous work experience do you have that demonstrates this?
- Outline these in one paragraph if possible.
- Make a list of the qualities the buyer is looking for.
- What qualities do you have that make you a good fit for the job?
- Outline them in one paragraph if possible.
- What relevant qualifications do you have?
- Outline these in one sentence.
- What questions has the buyer asked?
- Answer each question—providing a separate paragraph for each.

**Exercise 8.2**
While we need to be tailoring our responses for each project, it's okay to have a few standard bid outlines ready, to make the job easier.

Draft three different paragraphs that you could potentially use at the end of your proposals.

# 9

## Estimating Writing Projects

In this chapter we will:

1. Get down to basics and explore exactly how we estimate how much work is involved and how much we should charge.
2. Discuss what's a reasonable rate for a project; there are some details we need to understand.
3. Reveal how to calculate our basic rate. This is the minimum amount we need to learn to make freelancing a viable proposition.
4. Explore how to scope a piece of work.

## Estimating Rate and Work Effort

One of the most challenging tasks of establishing a successful freelance career is deciding how much to charge. It's not a question that will ever go away. When you're starting out, it's often a question of how much can you charge balanced against how much confidence you have. And then of course, as you gain experience you need to re-evaluate what you charge.

Unlike other businesses, a freelancer needs to approach this question with an element of flexibility. What you want to charge might not be feasible for a number of factors, such as the going market rate, the number of freelancers available and the amount of work about. But regardless, it is something that is negotiated and sometimes renegotiated with a client.

Setting and negotiating rates can seem complicated and intimidating but it doesn't need to be. A little preparation and you can go in ready, confident in the knowledge that you are charging a fair and reasonable price, and that you won't go hungry.

To decide what to charge you need to understand the different types of rates you will come across. There are typically four types of freelance writing rates:

- By the project, or flat rate
- By the hour
- By the word/page
- Retainer fee, for ongoing work

Let's start from the beginning and that's working out the number of hours you'll work.

Some basic calculations:

- There are 365 days in a year.
- If you're planning four weeks holiday a year (20 days), then you're down to 345 days.
- Take out public holidays (we'll used an estimate of eight days—this differs depending on location, so you will need to research this), then you're down to 337.
- Let's allow for some sick days (we'll use ten days for this exercise, but you might want to go with more or less) and that's 327.

Great! So that's 327 days available for us to earn money. Hang on a minute—as a freelancer, it's impossible to earn money for every hour we work because there must be time allocated to finding work, doing business administration and allowing for down time.

I typically allow for one day a week for my administration and finding work—so I take 20% off my number of days. If you're just starting out, it will be difficult to find work for five days a week, so I'd recommend you tread cautiously, and hope to work for three days a week. You might what to work with a different figure.

For the purposes of this exercise, I'll go with working three days a week, so that's 40% of my time. I will be working on my own administration and job finding but these are non-billable hours:

$$327 - (327 * 40\%) = 196 \text{ days}$$

Now you might want to have an hourly rate. You might think you can work eight hours a day, but is that reasonable? I typically go with seven hours. So, I have 196 days or 1372 hours a year to work.

> **Top Tip: Use a Freelancer Rate Calculator**
> Sites like this are a great place to start (and work with a number of different currencies, which is helpful). It's much too easy to guess a rate that we think is reasonable, but these calculators help us take into account other factors (such as needing unplanned time off):
> https://allfreelancewriting.com/freelance-hourly-rate-calculator/

## Your Basic Rate

While negotiation is a useful when bidding for work—you still need to be able to pay the bills and actually make a living, so before you start negotiating, you need to have a clear understanding of what you need to be earning to make this freelancing lark a going proposition. Your basic rate is the minimum about you can earn to make freelancing viable for you.

One way of calculating this is to take your previous or current salary—or the salary that you believe you need to earn as a freelancer—and divide it by the number of hours you plan on working.

Let's say for example, you want to earn £30,000 a year (we're using UK pounds for these examples, but it could just as well be in dollars or euros or other currencies and this will be impacted by your own country, standard of living and other such considerations—even inside countries there are variables. In the United Kingdom, living in London is more expensive than in Winchester; similarly New York and Utah). To achieve this figure of £30,000 a year based on my daily/hourly calculations above, I need to charge:

$$£30,000 / 196 = £153 \text{ a day or}$$
$$£30,000 / 1372 = £22 \text{ an hour}$$

These calculations are very rough and just a starting point. There are websites available, such as the **Freelancer Rate Calculator**, which incorporate average expenses and so on. Using my example of £30,000, and with the same number of billable hours, this website recommends a rate of £31 an hour. As we can see, there can be a lot of variation, so you need to try a few different methods and see what works for you. There are also other expenses you might need to consider if freelancing—for example, is your laptop reliable or do you need to invest in your setup? You might need to drive to client's sites so you'll have fuel costs.

Another useful website has been set up by writer and journalist Andrew Bibby, providing a UK **Freelance Ready Reckoner**. He has provided an equivalent gross salary, alongside what that would equate to as a total cost for an employer with a premise. He also lists the total cost for an employer without a premise, and then a recommended freelancer day rate:

http://www.andrewbibby.com/reckoner.html

For my example above of earning £30,000 a year, he calculates a total cost for the employer without a premise of £144 and recommends a freelancer day rate of £330.

If you're looking at some going rates on freelancing websites, £22 an hour is at the higher end—that's not to say that you can't ask for such a rate, especially if you have the experience; however, if you're just starting out, it might be a wakeup call that you're not going to make a fortune overnight. What are your options? Well, if you want to freelance, you'll need to consider if £30,000 (of whatever you've chosen) is realistic.

Another way of calculating this is to consider what you need to live (personal overheads), what it will cost to run your business (business overheads).

*Example*:

Personal overheads £15,000 + business overheads £5000.

Your basic rate (before tax) is £20,000/1372 = £15.

Don't forget tax—let's keep it simple at 20%.

£15 + 20% = £18—we have a basic rate of £18 that includes tax.

That doesn't mean we have to charge £18 per hour—but what it does mean is that when negotiating, we do not want to drop below £18 otherwise it's just not viable for us to pay our bills, run the business, pay our tax and live a little.

Now, you might be able to play with some of the variables—for example, your business overheads might be very low. Perhaps you're planning on working from home with your existing laptop. Maybe you need more than £15,000 a year to live, that's fine. Just play with the figures and see what is liable for you. But do think about overheads, electricity isn't free, heating isn't free. I don't heat the house during the day because I only need one space—like the kitchen table—to work so I wear lots of spare clothes, even wrap a blanket round my legs, two pairs of socks, you get the drift. The last thing you need is a good gig swallowed up by an unnecessary heating bill. But you do need to factor your bills into your potential income stream.

When you're starting out, your basic rate is important as it can be tempting to drop your rate to secure the work. It might be worth doing this, especially if you think there's the potential for future work—for example, if I was starting out and there was the potential that I could work for five days a week for six months, that's a pretty reasonable engagement—so I'd be prepared to go with lower (especially as my calculations were on the conservative side and were based on me only working three days a week). I could afford to drop.

What's important is that you have a rate that you are comfortable with and reflects your confidence in your skills. Work for less than the minimum wage (then you might ask yourself, is it really worth it), but equally, you're just not valuing your own skills and time. Better to earn what you believe your worth and you're deliver outstanding service.

As you gain experience, it's important to reassess your basic rate. I'd recommend at least every 6–12 months. As you grow in your skills and capabilities, your rate can reflect this. Though always bear in mind, it's a marketplace, and while I might want to charge £30 an hour, if no one's prepared to pay that, then I'll go hungry.

## Pricing Your Services

There are a couple of ways to approach putting a price on your services.

### Price per Project

With this approach you agree with the client the total cost for the project. Let's say it's for five web posts, each of 500 words, so that 2500 words in total, and you agree a total sum of £300. There is no requirement for you to detail how many hours you'll work on the project, but I would list the tasks this would include, such as research, writing, editing and then two reviews with the client. The big advantage to this approach for the freelancer is that you charge a fixed fee. If you decide to work at a fast pace and finish the work sooner than anticipated, and it won't affect the amount you earn for the job. It also means that if you finish the job early, you can delight your client but delivering early with no impact on what you earn.

With this approach, your speed, efficiency and knowledge, result in you earning more by freeing up your hours—rather than it being the client who benefits. Let's compare two freelancers—this is just a hypothetical example, and we'll assume they produce the same quality outcome. There's Andy—he's a bit slow and will take six hours to write a blog post. Then there's

Lisa—she's faster and will take only three hours. With a price per project approach, the client would pay £300 for the blog posts regardless of who does it and how long they take. If Andy takes the gig, he'll earn £50 an hour, whereas Lisa will earn £100 an hour—the client doesn't know and isn't interested in the freelancer's rate—they are paying for the end result, which is the five web posts.

## Price per Hour

With this approach you agree with the client the total hours you'll work and then your hourly rate. So instead of quoting £300 for my above example, I'd say that I'll work four hours on each post—so 20 hours, and charge £15 an hour. It works out to be the same amount, so what's the difference, I hear you ask? The big disadvantage this approach has for the freelancer, is that it gives the client the ability to negotiate your rate down. For example, now that they know that I'm working on the basic of four hours for each post, they might ask me to cut corners and spend only three hours on each. (And if you agree to this, what will typically happen is that you end up working the four hours anyway, because you don't want to compromise on quality). Or they might say that £15 an hour is more than they want to spend and try to negotiate you down. There is also the mindset for the freelancer that this is now a 20-hour job—and it's easy to allow a job to expand to fit what you agreed. It also means that if you do finish the job early and have a quick turnaround time, your client might then ask for a reduction.

Let's go back to our example of Andy and Lisa. If Andy wins the gig, he'll charge £10 and it will take him eight hours—for the five web posts it would cost the client £400. Lisa, on the other hand, charges £20 but it will take her four hours—for the five web posts, charging £400. The client doesn't want to pay Andy for eight hours when he can get Lisa for four hours—so they might try to get Andy to drop his hours down to four—thereby reducing his total amount to just £200, or likewise, dropping Lisa's rate. Either way, it's enabled the client to manipulate the variables to get the job done for less. If Lisa wants the gig, she's losing out because she's quick and efficient, meanwhile, Andy—who will deliver just as good a job, but will just take longer, is penalised. Though sometimes they have been known to split gigs. If Andy can't do both of the ones he's offered, he might suggest Lisa could do it—and of course that works both ways (and it's always good to have a couple of buddies you can work with, and likewise they you).

## Price per Word/Page

I've typically found that it's the very low paging writing gigs that want to pay per word or page. That said, some people do earn enough to make a living by such work. If it's regular than it's more about churn than quality. It's about turning out quantity rather than quality.

## Calculating Rates

### Per-Word Rates

Estimate how long it takes you to write 100 words in a typical service you're looking to offer—for example, you might choose writing a blog post. Convert this into hours. If it takes you 60 minutes to write a 500-word blog post, that equates to 500 words per hour. If your hourly rate is £20 per hour, divide that £20 by 500 words and you get a per word rate of £0.04 per word.

### Per-Page Rates

Similarly, estimate how many pages you can write per hour for that particular service offering, let's say a feature article this time. Divide your hourly rate by the number of pages you complete per hour. If it takes you 4 hours to write one for the article (including research and client consultation), you would divide your £30 hourly rate by 0.25 pages per hour and get a rate of per page of £120.

## The Marketplace

What you can charge will often come down to the marketplace and what your competition charges. A starting point is to look at other similar freelancers on freelancing platforms and see what they rate is.
There will always be variation depending on:

- the freelancer's experience and expertise;
- the field/area (e.g. I can charge more for my IT articles than my creative writing ones, simply because it's a specialised field and I have specialised knowledge);

- the services they provide—for example, will they be also conducting research? Editing? Proofreading? Revisions?
- Is it a niche field with limited writers available?
- Or is it a field saturated with writers? If that's the case, then despite your skills and knowledge, the client has the upper hand and can likely find someone who can deliver what they need for less.
- Complexity of the work involved. If I'm writing an article on the trends in social media for next year, I need to do extensive research, conduct analysis and draw conclusions. Whereas if I'm writing an article on how to make your Twitter profile stand out, it's going to need less upfront work.

This is also where your freelancing network comes in handy—compare and discuss rates, otherwise you're giving buyers the advantage.

But remember it's a global marketplace—you're not just competing with your local freelancers. You're up against people who are based in countries with potentially lower overhead costs and can therefore charge less.

Confidence is good, and certainly don't undersell your skills and services. But you also need to be realistic and understand where you fit in, compared to the competition. Are you nearer to the bottom or the top of the scale? The answer to this question determines how aggressively you can set your rates.

## Know Your Value

It's very difficult to negotiate a higher rate if you're competing in a saturated field. The best thing you can do is to try and place yourself in fields where there is less competition—so that means finding your niche areas. It might be in particular fields, such as my expertise in IT, or it can be in the services that you can provide. For example, you might be able to conduct data analysis.

You'll start to realise your value when buyers begin to specifically seek you out for projects. It could be because they've worked with you before or they've heard of you by reputation. Such clients are likely to pay more for your services because they believe you'll deliver. New clients are less willing because they don't yet know if you can do the work satisfactorily.

## Other Benefits?

When agreeing a rate with a client, it may not be completely a monetary transaction. It's possible there may be other benefits involved. For example:

- There might be a long-term potential for ongoing work.
- You might be writing a piece for a blog/website with a large following—so there are benefits to your reputation.
- The client might be flexible—meaning that you can fit the work in around your other commitments.
- You might use it to drive traffic to your own blog.
- The work is ongoing, pays reasonable and ensures you have some regular income.
- It's for a startup business and you know once they get off the ground, there will be more work for you.
- It's for a client with a strong network that you could benefit from.

## What to Charge?

This is a difficult one to advise on, as it will vary according to the freelancer's experience and area of expertise. But other factors will have an impact as well, such as the availability of other freelancers, the demand and supply of the marketplace, and the client's expectations.

The Editorial Freelances Association (US) provides advice on editorial rates: https://www.the-efa.org/rates/

The American Writers & Artists Institute provides a useful pricing guide for web copywriters: https://www.awai.com/web-marketing/pricing-guide/

The Australian Society of Authors provides recommended rates of pay on their website: https://www.asauthors.org/findananswer/rates-of-pay

The Society of Authors in the UK has a useful page on their website providing guidance on rates and fees: https://societyofauthors.org/Advice/Rates-Fees

The Society of Editors and Proofreaders (UK) has its suggested minimum rates for freelancers: https://www.ciep.uk/resources/suggested-minimum-rates/

The National Union of Journalists provides a *Freelance Fees Guide* and its London freelance branch also collects rates actually being paid. These are published in their *Freelancer* newsletter, available at: http://www.londonfreelance.org/rates/index.php

## Negotiating

While we don't particularly enjoy the job of negotiating, we've come to learn that it's an expected and necessary part of freelancing, especially when working with a new client. And actually, the vast majority of our clients have been reasonable and not expected us to work for an unreasonably low rate. But we have met clients that are only focused on rate, and the lowest possible, so we've walked away. Because of the nature of where we live, we will always charge more on a global marketplace, than other freelancers. So, there is no point trying to compete with other freelancers that are much, much cheaper. If a client is only focused on getting the lowest possible price, we're never going to win. But we've also discovered that clients have sometimes had their fingers burnt from cheap freelancers that just didn't deliver. You get what you pay for, and all of that. Ultimately, they are looking for a quality job done for a reasonable price.

> **Top Tip: Don't Shy Away from Talking About Money**
>
> Try to establish a client's budget before talking rates. This will help ensure you're in a reasonable ballpark. Too far out and you're wasting your time. It's not a pleasant subject and none of us really like talking dollar (or pound, euro, rupee, yen etc.) but it's business and important and the client will expect it from a professional writer.

## Scoping the Work

You can't price a project unless you understand the scope of what is required. If you make this mistake, you may disappoint the client by delivering something other than what they want and have to spend extra (likely unpaid) time, to rectify the issues. A proposal (see the previous chapter) seems to define what the job entails, and this includes scoping out what is, and sometimes what isn't included. If you can't define that yet, come to a temporary agreement with the understanding that a firm contract will be agreed when you reach the next stage.

Once a proposal has been accepted, ensure there is formal agreement in place—for a small piece of work, this might be an email, but if it's longer, a formal contract.

## Have Some Standard Guides

As you're setting your rates, you'll want to think about the kinds of projects you'll be asked to take on and estimate how many hours it will take from start to finish. What kind of writing will you be producing? Web articles? Newsletters? Website content? Estimate the amount of time each will take you.

Don't forget to include non-writing time. Many beginning freelance writers only consider the time to write the piece, and not the research, revision, or editing, which can add hours to the amount of time you're working on a project. For example, if you're paid £20 per article, and can write it in an hour, you'd earn £20 per hour. But if you have to research, and it takes an additional hour, now you're earning half, or £10 per hour. Add a further hour for editing and now your hourly rate is down to £6.60. If the client then wants further changes you could be looking at £5 an hour.

## Pricing a Job

It can be difficult to try and price a large or complex piece of work, because it's difficult to ascertain exactly what it entails. In this instance, try and break it down into its constituent parts—and keep breaking it down until you have a piece of work you can estimate. With this list of parts, you can then estimate the time to complete each (and include some contingency). Add these together and include an overriding contingency which gives you some wiggle room during negotiations. Clients typically like to feel that they've got the price down a bit (we all like to get a good deal, right?), so this is where your contingency helps.

Remember, your basic rate is the lowest you're typically prepared to go, unless there are some pretty good other benefits on offer.

You'll also need to bear in mind how much you want the work; can you afford to turn it away for a slight drop in your rate? Perhaps you've got plenty of work already, so taking on a low-paying gig doesn't make a lot of sense. Perhaps you've just completed a well-paying gig so can afford to be a bit more lenient for the sake of securing a new client (and you can always renegotiate your rate again for the next piece of work). Consider your situation and negotiate away. Just remember caution—if negotiating down becomes a habit and you are regularly prepared to accept lower than your basic rate, it's not a viable proposition to make a living from.

## Going Under Your Base Rate?

If a client attempts to negotiate below your base rate, you have three options:

1. Grin and bear it.
2. Refuse and walk away.
3. Negotiate and reduce the scope of works.

Option 1 is only to be considered if other benefits related to the work outweigh the difference the paying rate and your base rate. I have a client who is a good example of this. They pay me a little under my base rate, but they list my details on their website which has been good for promoting my services.

Option 2 should be taken if you are comfortable that you should not charge lower than your base rate for the proposed work—and the other benefits don't stack up either.

Option 3 is a compromise. Perhaps you can deliver the first of an ongoing delivery of blog posts (for example). This way you can prove your skills (and also test how much time it will take you). You then have the option of walking away—as does the client—or renegotiating the rate. In my experience, clients like this option as it puts them in the driving seat and they can decide.

## Retainers

Retainers are more likely to occur if the work is particularly large and requires a lot of upfront investment of your time. If a client isn't keen on this, you could propose a shorter payment period over a probation period. This could then be followed up with a long-term agreement/contract.

## Rates Are Not Set in Stone

Setting your rate is an ongoing process that you go through with each of your clients. Get it wrong and it's not the end of the world. You can always renegotiate the next piece of work, and it's all experience you can apply when your next client comes along.

# Getting Better at Estimating

It's never easy trying to estimate a piece of work, especially if the client is vague about what they want, and the work just seems to keep escalating. So how can you get better? Here's some tips:

- It's tempting, when you finish a project, to rush off to the next one. Allow yourself some time to go back and analyse some of the project information.

How long did it really take you? (be honest!) Keep a spreadsheet with some basics on it. You might be allowing yourself two hours for research, but if you end up spending four hours all up, on a regular basis, then you need to be revising your initial estimates.
- Don't be shy! Share, share and share. Ask your freelancing and writing community how long standard activities take them. I was rather embarrassed to ask for more than a couple of hours researching when I started out, until I realised that other writers are doing just that.
- Experience. It's a pretty obvious thing to say, but the more you do something, you get a gut free for how long it will take. Client's expectations that are not realistic will set off alarm bells. It's an instinct that grows the more experience you get. But this is where your network can help—just a few reliable freelance buddies can really help give you advice and support.

## Some Useful Guides

### Writingassist.com

These guys have really useful guidelines for the tasks involved for different types of writing projects and time estimates:
https://www.writingassist.com/pdfs/EstimatingWritingProjects_V51.pdf

## Key Chapter Points

- Know your basic rate before you begin negotiating your rate—calculate in your overheads and don't forget time spend on finding work, administration etc. Understand that this is the minimum you need to receive to make freelancing viable—which there might be an exceptional situation where it is beneficial to accept lower, in most instances, your basic rate is the minimum you should accept.
- What service value are you offering? What do our competitors charge? How competitive is the marketplace? How much demand is there for work of this type? Are there any indirect benefits relating to working with this client?
- Do some research and see what other similar freelancers' charge.
- Know your place in the market—if you have a niche skill you can potentially charge towards the higher end.

- Be flexible—your base rate is a guide to apply in most situations but there will be occasions where the other benefits make it acceptable to go under your base rate.
- Get comfortable talking about money—this will get easier over time.
- Try to establish a client's budget before talking rates.

## Exercise 9.1

Jennifer wants to move into freelancing and is trying to work about how much she should charge.

Here are some basics:

- Her personal yearly overheads: rent is £7500, living expenses are £5500, other expenses are £3000.
- Her anticipated business overheads are £250 a month.
- If she earns over £11,000, she'll need to pay tax of 20% on the amount over £11,000.
- She'd like to work four days a week.
- She'd like to go on a six weeks' holiday a year.
- She figures she'll work public holidays.
- She doesn't fall sick much, so reckons five days a year are enough.

Calculate Mary's base rate.

## Exercise 9.2

Jaime has found a very tempting project on a freelance platform. It is to write two articles of 1000 words and the buyer is offering to pay £150. They estimate the work will take one hour to research, two hours to write and one hour to edit, for each article.

Should Jaime bid for the work?

Has Jaime forgotten anything in the calculation of four hours for each article?

# 10

# Planning and Managing Writing Projects

In this chapter we will:

1. Cover when we need to plan.
2. Look at how the planning process works.
3. Consider risks, issues and stumbling blocks—and how to deal with them.
4. Discuss tools that can help us all.

## Planning Writing Projects

If we plan before we write, then there's a much better chance that we'll write clearly and coherently. Without a plan, then experience tells us any project can easily miss the mark. You might get lucky, of course, but why leave it to chance? As a freelancer, it can result in spending a lot longer than you'd estimated for the work. Sometimes even affect the standard of the work because it's not as ordered or well-structured as it should be. What's the problem, so long as you deliver? As a freelancer, you can just put in the extra time. That's true but think back to our earlier chapter on making freelancing a viable proposition, which will pay all our bills and more. That's not going to happen if you have to effectively keep throwing in extra, unpaid hours. Or end up working at an hourly rate far below what your work is worth, or that you can survive on (remember your basic in Chap. 9?) But there are other consequences. There are plenty of freelancers out there, so if you disappoint a client, they will just as likely go elsewhere. Or your article might get published (actually this is probably the worst one) and the readers will vote with their feet (metaphorically). If your client's website, for example, suddenly gets a lot of negative comments due to your piece, it's not great for your reputation (or your confidence).

So, you can skip this chapter if you wish but that's a pretty risky strategy. Just like going off on vacation or building a house extension, planning is required (unless of course, you want to spend your holiday missing that attraction because it turns out it was shut on Mondays! Or building that extension which has to be pulled down because, umm … you didn't get planning permission, or the foundations are too weak for your two-level structure).

There are different stages in the life of a project where we need to plan:

- Before we even have the job:
  We need to provide an estimate of time and cost for a project. It's a hazardous game to play, simply to have a guess and hope to renegotiate later. Even if the client agrees, they won't be impressed. When getting started, come up with a few basic plans for how long it will take you to write the typical projects you're planning to go for. For example, you might say for a 500-word article, you'll include: two hours for research, two hours for writing and two hours for editing. To ensure I have some contingency, I'll have a buffer—say, an additional two hours. So, I might quote between six and eight hours, depending on the information provided and the amount of research required. That way I have some wriggle room.
- When you get the job:
  You'll probably get a lot more information at this stage. It turns out that article on how to help your family build up resistance to the common cold this winter, actually needs significant research. Rather than going into a panic, I can explain to the client that my estimate was for two hours' research, and I can provide a basic article with this amount of research. If they want me to do a more detailed piece, then it's additional work. With this approach you give the client the choice—go with your two hours' research and have a piece based on limited research or decide to go with a more in-depth article.
- Throughout the project:
  Projects are dynamic events therefore your planning needs to allow for this. Clients will change their minds (frustrating I know, but it's just the way it is) so you'll need to be flexible. Does it work the other way around? I'm afraid it doesn't. While you need to be adaptable, you can't expect the same back—after all, they are paying for your services. Another better paying job comes along? Personally, a commitment is a commitment, and that small-time client might just be my biggest next year (it's happened). If I'm contracted to deliver a small project, the better paying one just has to wait. Painful as it is to turn work down, some clients are impressed with such professional behaviour and might be able to wait or work with you in the

future. But if I really want both jobs, I might decide to work overtime, or I might work with another freelancer (it's situations like this where your freelance network is invaluable!)

It does not do to leave a live dragon out of your calculations, if you live near one.
J.R.R. Tolkien

Dragons, I hear you exclaim. This is professional writing, not fantasy and dragons are not going to feature heavily surely. What I think Tolkien was telling us, is that we need to plan ahead and understand what our potential risks are. It's about understanding what needs to be done, where the weak points are, so that we can prevent the weak points, or the dragons, coming back to trip us up. I recently won some work for a client in the travel industry. I've written travel pieces before, but it was a very different approach and a location I wasn't familiar with. To be honest, it gave me a few sleepless nights as it was out of my comfort zone. So, what did I do? I came up with a plan. Now I am doing more work for the client because the travel industry encountered a dragon called Pandemic, which they have had to factor into their calculations.

In the same way, all freelancers should become excellent planners. Rather than getting tripped up by potential clients and future readers, they can try to stay one step ahead. By so doing, they can try to anticipate any objections or arguments they might have. Of course, you can't anticipate everything, but there's a good chance you'll cover most. You can also build in contingency if you think something has a reasonable chance of occurring. If you can anticipate possible disagreements or future hurdles, you can make some choices. If they are serious threats that are very likely to occur, then you can build in additional steps to prevent them from happening, or you can discuss it with your client, and should it come up, then it's no surprise to either party.

Benefits of planning and managing your projects:

- Happy clients (this is the most important one). A happy client is more likely to give you more work and recommend you to others.
- Time spent planning is never wasted. Much like writing software code, planning your writing before you start will save you time and energy.
- Avoiding disappointment. There's nothing more disappointing than writing something which you think is brilliant, only for the client to say it's not what they want. Make what they want brilliant.
- Better-quality writing. Planning ahead will mean that you are confident what you're writing will fit the bill when it comes to the requirements. You'll also be more relaxed because you know you've built in time to properly edit it, once you're done.

- Becoming more efficient. Rather than leaping in and hoping for the best, if you break any task down into smaller, manageable components, you're better able to see if it's going to be achievable.
- Being more relaxed. It might seem strange, but actually knowing that you have a plan, and seeing that a task is manageable in bite-sized chunks, takes the pressure of. It's often the unknown which makes us stressed. But if we can see what needs to be done, and that it's manageable in the time we have available, we can relax and get on with the task at hand.
- Realistically know what you can and can't commit to. It will happen… that day when a load of work comes knocking on your door. It's tempting to say yes to everything—but if you do so, not knowing that you have the capacity to take it all on—you're creating a messy situation, one where you're very stressed and clients are disappointed. Best all-around to avoid this happening.
- Knowing your deadlines! Be prepared so these don't sneak up on you, causing a late-night working session, or worse still, the need to disappoint a client.
- Gives focus and routine. It's all too easy to think that you have plenty of time and that something can wait until tomorrow—unless you have a schedule and realise that if you don't get the research done today, then the whole project will slip and then there will be no time for rewriting and editing.
- Provides reminders. This helps us focus on what needs to be done today. It's all too easy to do the tasks we enjoy and ignore those we don't like. That doesn't work when you're freelancing—you need to do those tasks that must be done today!
- Staying on top of clients and projects. So, you can send out your invoices on time and chase those that are tardy.
- Budgeting. Yep, it's not pleasant, but it needs to be done otherwise freelancing just isn't for you. And you can't budget if you don't project manage.

## Planning Process

### Getting Started: Identify the What, Who, Why and How

#### What Are You Really Writing About?

The most important question for you to answer, before you even begin to write the piece, is "What's your piece about?"

Try to answer that roughly one to three sentences. If the client or the spec are vague, you can easily go back with a short email, asking for their confirmation you're on the right track. Remember, Einstein said. "If you can't explain it to an eight-year-old, you don't understand it."

**Who Cares?**

Who are the target audience? The client might have explicitly told you, and you can of course ask them, but it's possible they haven't thought about this (sadly) or are a bit vague. If that's the case, do some research. If the piece is for a company's website, take a look at it as see if you can determine who they are targeting. Often though, you will find the client vague, and it might be up to you to suggest they may be missing a trick. A client sees his product and not always those who will appreciate it. Who could have predicted Facebook would leave its teenage users behind as their parents moved in.

**Why Is This Piece Needed?**

What is the client hoping to achieve with your piece of writing? It might be to gain more customers but often it goes beyond this. Sometimes it's to inform—for example, they might be reviewed as an authority in their field, and they want their website to publish market leading articles. Or they may want to break into a new target market—let's say they are a traditional walking shoe company, who currently sell well to the middle-aged (well-heeled—forgive the pun) market, but they now want to attract a younger age group. Maybe the website's blog hasn't been very active of late, so they're keen to show the company is up to date with their industry. This one shouldn't be too difficult to answer—and if your client is struggling to answer this, well … it's not a good sign!

**How Will This Piece Be Delivered?**

I was recently asked to deliver a new website, but actually after discussion with the client, it changed format. After exploring what it was and the client's aim, my suggestion that it would be better delivered as an online magazine, was taken up. It's much better suited to their requirements, they'll be able to manage it easier, and it's become a good promotion tool for them—they just hadn't known about it as an option before I suggested it. From my experience, if you can see a better way of doing something—speak up. Websites are a good tool, fine for quick reference but a magazine can sometimes say much more. If the client doesn't want to hear it, that's fine, I'm happy to deliver exactly what they want—but at least I've given them the option. And if someone else comes along later and asks, why didn't we do it differently? Well, it was their choice.

## Step-by-Step Planning for Writing Projects

Because I've freelanced a long time, and have done similar projects before, I'm getting better at my estimating. That's not to say I don't get it wrong sometimes, and of course sometimes I get my fingers burned. But the better I became, the more work I got. I found that I was winning more bids and tenders than I was losing—when it came to my time and estimating. So long as the majority of my projects are coming in shorter or the same as I estimated, I know I'm on track. And the odd case, where I get it wrong—I can live with that because I have some built in contingency—and time gained from unused contingency elsewhere.

A writing project can include any number of tasks. These might include:

- Researching

  - a library database search/catalogue search to find relevant journal articles or books
  - online articles and posts

- Reading and taking notes
- Brainstorming and idea generation
- Analysing data and looking for information
- Planning the structure of your article
- Interviews

## Discussions

- Drafting and rewriting
- Editing and proofreading

Here is a basic outline that I use to plan my writing projects. Feel free to borrow, adopt and improve on it:

1. Brainstorm ideas—mind mapping might work for you. Outcome is a list of possible ideas, approaches and topics for the piece. Initially capture as many ideas as possible, without worrying about structure. Think of key words and topics that could give direction to your reading and research. You might want to use images, diagrams, tables and flowcharts. It can help to discuss your ideas with someone else.
2. Put the ideas into some sort of order (it might be most important to least important, could even just be chronological).
3. What ideas really stand out? Which ones are unique and possibly less know?
4. What ideas need more research? Perhaps you think writing about dog leashes is a great idea for that dog website, but perhaps that subject was written about last week in *This Dog* magazine.
5. Shuffle—you haven't written anything yet so you can play around easily. Just because events might happen chronologically doesn't mean that you have to always write them that way. Can you order your ideas in a way that hooks your reader and holds their interest?
6. Write your first draft.
7. Look at it from a content perspective. Is it too light weight in a particular area and some additional research would really help?
8. Produce your next draft.
9. Read it out loud—look for any mistakes—and edit, edit, edit… and don't this last thing at night. Even if you have a tight deadline, giving yourself a break until next morning will let you see it in new light, and you won't be so tired. Take it from both of us—editing late at night when you're tired is never a good idea.
10. Finalise your piece. Polish and really work your craft. Make your writing leap off the page and punch your reader on the nose (okay, perhaps I'm getting carried away, but you know what I mean).

## Keeping Track of Project Information

### For Each Client

- Their details (address, emails, banking etc.)
- Their projects
- Their invoices

## For Each Project

- Date assigned
- Internal deadline—my personal deadline
- Client deadline—this is the deadline the client set
- Finished project
- First edit
- Run project through a grammar and spelling checker (such as Grammarly or ProWritingAid)
- Run project through a plagiarism checker (such as CopyScape)
- Peer review required
- Final proofread
- Submitted to client
- Invoiced sent
- Payment amount received

## For Each Task

- Duration—how long it will take.
- Effort—this can be the same as the duration, but it can differ—for example, something might be quick to complete, but you might need to wait for something from the client, so the actual duration is longer.
- Dependencies—for example, you can't start to write until you do the research, or maybe you need to interview someone before you can finalise the piece.
- Milestones and deadlines—these are dates that must be met.
- Who needs to do the task?

# Project Management and Writing Projects

Managing your writing projects effectively is just as important as the writing itself. As we've already covered, a freelancer has to become efficient in many fields: marketing, budgeting, financial management, client relationship management, accounting and so on. Managing via an old-fashioned spreadsheet is one thing but there are some tools to help you keep things on track and organised. Thankfully, there are a number of project management tools can help make some of these tasks much easier. This isn't an exhaustive list, but more provided to give you a flavour for the types of products available.

Products come and go, so it's possible some of the products we list today are no longer around tomorrow. We're providing these as a list to help get you started with an understanding of the types of products on the market. But also do your research and we are not advocating any of these.

## Asengana

These guys promote their tool as the first project management platform for writers. It uses Kanban and Burndown chart modules to make you more efficient and hopefully improve your estimating (sounds like a good thing to me). Workflow based, this can help to understand what can get done in the time you have available.

## Basecamp

Basecamp is another project management application that centralises all information and communication for projects that involve multiple (and often remote) contributors. The software includes features such as discussion threads, calendars, uploading of project files and to-do lists.

## Evernote

Research is an important aspect to many projects. To help organise the vast array of information gathered during this phase, writers can store their files using their filing systems (can get messy) or they can use a tool such as Evernote. Even the free version of this tool makes it easy to collect, edit, and manage notes. You can also embed images, links, and voice memos. Research can be grouped together for a specific project in a specific notebook, keeping everything together. There is the facility to tag notes with keywords for easy retrieval later on. I particularly like the feature that allows you to take screen captures of web pages that you see (all too often I've noted down an address, for it to be gone when I've returned to it later on).

## FreshBooks

The great thing about this application is that it combines project management and billing (a big bonus for the freelancer who is great at getting the work done, but less efficient and keeping on top of sending out those pesky invoices). FreshBooks includes invoice and expense tracking, time tracking, estimating and collaboration tools.

## Podio

Another project management application that comes with project templates, which can help you get started.

## Redbooth

This application is good if you're managing a lot of deadlines. It's a bit like have an assistant who is reminding you of what needs your urgent attention.

## Taskboard

This is a completely free, open-source project management application. If you're looking for pretty standard project management functionality, this could fit the bill and it has some nice automatic update features.

## Thrive

The application was designed for freelancers, so understands the need to work around clients and projects. It has built in functionality to help you analyse client information, such as understanding who your most profitable ones are.

## Trello

A very popular task management tool, Trello is great for freelancers, enabling them to organise their projects. The tool is organised around boards (you can use for clients) and cards (can be used for your projects). The freelancer can then attach various details, such as to do lists, deadlines, documents, ideas and so on.

## Ulysses III

Ulysses III is a project management software program designed for writers, and especially research heavy projects such as manuals or novels. A single file contains all the documentation for a project, such as revision history, embedded media, and notes or annotations, in addition to the actual content.

## Wrike

Another organisation took, this allows you to set up folders, create tasks and give them deadlines. Its standout feature is being able to track how much time you really spend on a task (could be very revealing and none of us want to admit how much time it really takes us!).

## Do You Really Need a Fancy Tool?

No, it's definitely not a necessity, especially when just starting out. I survived for many years with my Excel spreadsheets, though it became too difficult to manage when I began juggling multiple projects and clients. Tools can help and my advice is to look around and try and free versions. Often this can be enough for a small freelancing business.

# Key Chapter Points

- Don't underestimate the value of planning. The more we plan, the better we are at estimating our work and ensuring we can charge the correct amount. Rush into a project, and it will likely take a lot longer, have a lot more challenges and hurdles, and it can lead to unhappy clients.
- Planning can feel daunting, but it's really not. It's about taking the time to understand a task and breaking it down into achievable chunks. Once any project is broken down into realistic and definable components, then we can relax in the knowledge we know what we need to do, and we've given ourselves the right amount of time to do it.
- Don't forget contingency! Things can go wrong—my network disappeared last week, and there wasn't anything I could do about it. If there had been a deadline to meet that day, I would have been in a pickle. But not if I'd allowed for a day's contingency to get my work in (and it's a good tip to still being able to work offline. A good plan allows you to keep working)
- Keep track of information. This saves time and avoids the risk of costly mistakes. Such as not being able to bill the client correctly because you don't know how much time you spent on a project. Sure, you can guess it,

but that's not a viable long-term strategy, and sometimes clients like to know such analytics. If you don't have them, you can end up looking very amateurish.
- Take advantage of tools available on the market. Many have free entry-level options. They might not give you all the bells and whistles, but they can definitely help.

**Exercise 10.1**
Below are two typical opportunities you might find available online. You're going to bid for these but first you need to come up with a plan so you can estimate the work involved. They are pretty brief, but that's because many online job descriptions will be. It's ok to have questions:

**Writing for a food/cooking website**
**Experience level:** entry
**Estimated duration:** ongoing

I have a food website that I would like to have some content written. I need an introductory paragraph, and some articles on food preparation, and a recipes section. I'd also like to have a blog, with regular posts on a weekly basic. Because it's about food and cooking, I need instructions written clearly. The pieces will be between 300 and 500 words long. I will require you to do the necessary research before writing.

Come up with a list of tasks needed to complete this piece of work.
What questions do you have to be able to finalise your plan?

**Writing a blog for social media**
**Experience level:** expert
**Estimated duration:** less than a week

I need a copywriter who can write articles for a blog and content for a website. The writer will be given topics and some initial information but some additional may be required.

Come up with a list of tasks needed to complete this piece of work.
What questions do you have to be able to finalise your plan?

# 11

## The Editing Process

In this chapter we will:

1. Think about editing.
2. Look at narrative voice.
3. Consider active or passive prose.
4. Ponder punctuation.
5. Think about writing right.

At the beginning of this book we said,

Writing is probably one of the most important developments in communication mankind ever invented. Word of mouth knowledge soon became knowledge transcribed, on papyrus, stone and anything else we could get our hands on to hand down, generation by generation. Bees have been present in human history for over 6,000 years and we know how to get their honey without stinging ourselves because someone already wrote down telling us how.

Imagine if we had written,

Writing is brilliant. How would we communicate without it? We can't exactly 'talk' to everyone. We don't know who invented it but thank goodness he did. Of course, saying 'he' assumes it was a man. It could have been a woman. After all, this book is written by two people and one of them is a woman. Though of course in Genesis 2: 22 the person who wrote the Old Testament gave these words, 'And from the rib that the LORD God had taken from the man, He made a woman and brought her to him.' Now who would have written that but a man? (What do you mean, you don't agree? Well even early writing has critics) Anyway, back to 'writing', it's a very fine invention, don't you think?

Both paragraphs actually say similar things, which is that writing is very important. However, clearly the second paragraph wanders off topic (maybe just a little). You might even find the second paragraph more interesting to read, in a strange kind of way. Nevertheless, we need to ask, is it doing the job it should? Well, the editor will say no. We know this as we write it. It's flabby and meanders and full of information that doesn't have to be there. And yet it helps us to explain the role of the editor because we can see all the things that shouldn't be there. It's easy to say editing is about checking the typos and the grammer [*sic*] and the spelling (see how easily we segued into that little joke after misspelling 'grammer'—ask yourself, did we really need it?). Editing is about *getting all the right words in the right order*. Take it from us, though, very few of us hit that target straight away, indeed if at all. By the time you read this, our edit will have been edited by a professional editor appointed by our publisher. And thank goodness too, editing is harder than it looks. It becomes easier with practice, though, and there are some golden rules, which we can bring to you here.

## Thinking About Ways to Edit

Editing is the literally the process of making changes to a text before publishing it. But this doesn't tell us a lot; for example, it may involve:

- removing or adding copy to meet a word count (which is very important for the professional writer);
- making your sentences stronger, clearer and succinct;
- restructuring paragraphs or sections so that the 'story' they tell is maximised to the best effect;
- making sure the ideas being presented flow cogently and rationally, and make sense;
- making sure enough background information is provided (without overwhelming the foreground information);
- making sure the focus is clear; and
- adding in subheadings or sentences to clearly signpost the foreground information being presented.

Once you have taken these points into account its ready to be proofread and edited. It would be great then just to pass it on for someone else to do this—it's a known fact that none of us are the best editors of our own work. However, that is a luxury we can't afford, so it's up to you to consider the best way to approach it. If we can slip in a *huge* tip (especially for long pieces), it is edit 'hard copy'—an old-fashioned paper-and-pencil approach, checking the spelling, grammar and references, as appropriate. But these pointers are worth considering:

- Editing is an art form perfected by people who do it for a living. And like playing the piano, you need to learn how to do it well. Everyone can play notes, but you have to play the right notes in the right order. You also have to practise. Get into good habits by mentally editing everything you read. Does that newspaper column read correctly? Could that email from your best friend have been written better? You don't have to tell him or her you are editing their message; it's just an exercise. Did the letter from the gas company responding to your enquiry make sense (I had one recently which was appalling)? You don't have to correct it for them, but you could see how it could have been written better. Get into the habit of checking this kind of copy; it doesn't take long, and you end up doing it almost subconsciously. These are things to think about, especially when it comes to editing your own work.
- Chop up long sentences—keep them short and precise. You may have written a sentence which, for the most part, is written well and punctuated appropriately, with the correct attention paid to grammar and even a quaint, lyrical flourish just to embellish the point being made—like this one. But did I need to write like that? Most newspapers deliver short sentences. Five or six words is good. You only need one qualifier, an adjective. Ask yourself why. It's because the sentence is there to deliver a short, sharp message. Read newspapers, you will see this. Read the BBC website, their writers are masters of the economical sentence.

Many longer sentences are grammatically correct. This is absolutely true. However, they tend to be less precise. They tend to hold more information. They tend to be a bit dull for the person who just needs to 'find things out'.

So, the advice is cut out commas. Cut out tautologies (though I do laugh at 'it's déjà vu all over again') Cut out adverbs (ruthlessly). For example, 'talking quietly' can easy drop to one word, 'whispers'. 'You get the idea', he *said weakly* or *he sighed* (which is the best signoff here). In fact, adverbs weaken sentences because they are a lazy way of passing over descriptive images. Be positive, shaking your fist is a stronger image than gesturing angrily. Another way of thinking about this is simply, cut out the '–lys'.

## Narrative Voice

What has this got to do with editing you might ask? Well, actually a lot. The best piece of advice is to settle on a narrative voice appropriate to every piece you write. Sounds obvious, doesn't it?

- You will be required to write in many styles. It will usually be necessary (and indeed normal) to use both first and second person. However, that can create its own problems. For example, you might start your introduction talking about yourself (or impersonating your client's voice):

> Hi,
> Jack here. Look at our new range of Sensational Socks …

The personal touch from the first-person personal point of view is engaging and allows you (or jack in this case) to engage as though the customer is a friend (notable IKEA do this all the time—when I was writing this, this email came into my inbox:

> IKEA Family ikea@news.email.ikea.co.uk
> Andrew, we know it's been tricky to get a head start on summer this year. Well, with IKEA now open again it's time to squeeze every last drop out of the season ahead. Take advantage of summer with ….

From an editorial perspective this familial, personal touch sends out a good message, personalised and reads like an invitation. However, all too often it changes when addressing the product. Sometimes the tone switches and not for the better. Taking Jack's socks again. If we move into the impersonal, almost second person, we can demonstrate:

> Hi,
> Jack here. Look at our new range of Sensational Socks.
> Taking Blake's work on The Beatles' *Sergeant Pepper* album as inspiration, the striking colours and sixties collage influence will bring colour to any outfit. Reasonably priced and free delivery, etc. ….

Let's try that again:

> Hi,

Jack here. Look at our new range of Sensational Socks.

We share a love of sixties style. So, we have taken inspiration from Peter Blake's work on the Beatles' *Sergeant Pepper* album to bring you something really exciting. The striking colours and sixties collage influence will bring colour to any outfit. We wondered how we managed without them. We are sure you will too.

All for a reasonable price, straight to your door, etc. ….

The more serious switch halfway thought the first example stands in stark contrast to the second, where the first-person familiar is maintained in the use of 'we' and a happy smiley address.

In truth, both are correct and there is little wrong with either of them. But if you start in the informal you should keep it that way. And don't think this just refers to something as flippant as Sergeant Pepper socks. My bank writes to me in a very similar way. They treat me like I am part of their family, or at least community.

## Negative Positive or Should That Be Positive Negative?

As we have shown above, Jack is telling you what the socks are. There is a positive statement. They are socks influenced by the work of artist Pater Blake during his Sergeant Pepper period. Don't tell a customer what the product isn't. Make sure your work is edited to tell them what it is.

Don't say,

'Don't wear those old socks. Not your every day, run of the mill socks ….'

Rather say,

'Chuck out those old, every day socks. We have something special for you.'

Using negative words like 'not', don't, shouldn't, can't or another such words tend to inflect a negative idea in the presentation. The piece should say what to do, not what not to do.

## Active Voice

Avoid using a passive narrative voice—and you really should read up on this. A passive voice constructs a sentence where the subject and not the object become the focus. Think about it in defensive terms:

- That article had been written when I was young and inexperienced.

  Activate the voice by removing the coy and apologetic 'had been':
- I wrote the article when I was young and inexperienced.

  A passive voice would say:
- A candle was left burning all night

  Activate the voice by identifying the point of the statement:
- You left a candle burning all night
- He left a candle burning all night
- Somebody left a candle burning all night.

The first, passive voice, hints at 'I wonder who?' the active voice points the finger, 'You left it burning.' It's obvious in selling brochures. Let's go back to the snazzy socks and decide which the passive is and which the active:

- Who loves our new snazzy socks?
- You will love our new socks!

## I Would Like To

While we are writing this, the Covid daily bulletins are on the radio and television. During these bulletins, members of the press and media are allowed to ask questions. Have you noticed how many people begin a question with, 'I would like to ask …' Think about this and then extend the idea, 'I would like to tell you …' 'I would like to say …' 'May I just say …' 'Let me tell you …' Why ask for permission. Just say it. I heard an internationally recognised, political commentator on the BBC say out loud, 'Mr Prime Minister, I would like to ask …' What? Why? Why ask for permission? Why not just say, 'Mr Prime Minister, do you know what you are doing?' Straight out, to the point, precise, succinct and no words wasted. Jack said,

Jack here, look at our new range of Sensational Socks.'

He didn't need permission by saying,

*Jack here, I would like to tell you* about our new socks.

Or,

*Jack here, may I just say*, our new socks are fabulous!

What is the point of us writing, '*May we just say*, there is no point in wasting time on lengthening the sentence and prevaricating on the message we are trying to tell you here. When what we want to say is, cut to the chase. Don't prevaricate, get to the point of what you want to say or what you want to ask. Besides it leads to all kinds of confusion too. The policeman who says, 'Can I ask where you're going?' This could legitimately be answered, 'Of course you can, ask away.' Okay, perhaps you're not going to get into that discussion, but you see what we mean. A simple and direct question is always best. 'Can I ask when you last changed your socks?' might sound polite in conversation. But in copy, well, even using a negative to drive it is better than that, 'Isn't it time you had new socks?' Though of course we would have gone for, 'Time you had new socks! Here you go, I have just the pair you need.'

And while we are about it there are two words you should think about their correct usage. You deserve these snazzy socks as you are the best. Should be, 'You deserve these snazzy socks because you are the best.' If you need to use 'as' then it could be, 'As it happens, we're having a sale.' All too often 'as' is used in place of 'because' and it weakens the delivery of the message.

The other word is 'that'. 'I am certain that her eyes are blue …' is grammatically fine. But why not just cut to the point. 'I am certain her eyes are blue.' It reads more succinctly and the word 'that' is superfluous.

## Punctuation

When I am reading for fun, I like writers that makes me think. This usually means encountering sentences with weighty concepts, lots of hyphens and semi-colons. Not so much Henry James, who can be a tad over the top, but Salman Rushdie or Ali Smith; Luce Irigaray or Slavoj Žižek, whose writing is all about exploring ideas. And in their writing, an authoritative hyphen here and there, a thought-provoking, broken-backed sentence using brackets, semicolons and the odd codicil can really allow the idea to be developed. Such sentences make demands on the reader. They are sentences that say; sit down and read me, think about what I am saying, consider the ideas I am proposing (whether you agree with them or not is irrelevant at this stage) before asking you to go on with your reading—are you following me? However, as can be seen, they do tend to go on and can be hard work. You really should be thinking about punctuating sentences with full stops. Make them short and sharp. Punchy, impactful sentences work better. Professional writing isn't an ekphrastic poem describing the Shield of Achilles or the philosophy of the Western world.

Keep sentences short and sharp. It's the best advice.

## Word Smart

Writing is about getting the right words in the right order. Sometimes we have to consider if the words being 'right' is enough. There are many things to consider here. For example:

- Profanities—We don't have to look very far for a swear word these days. Television and newspaper journalism is rife with them. Nevertheless, there is never really any need for them. Indeed, often, such as some I have seen in The Guardian newspaper recently, they are gratuitous and often just there to support limp jokes. Be careful and consider your readership is the rule of thumb.
- Blasphemy—in the name of goodness (I know I could have said God and worse). There will be some who take no offence at all. However, you do need to respect those who will. As with profanity, it's usually just loose talk, careless words and a good editor won't let them sneak into the copy they are presenting. Its sheer common sense—don't alienate your reader.
- Race, gender, sexuality and minorities, including minority ideas and concepts—just because you might have opinions about women, gay people and so on, you can't assume everyone else shares them. Also be careful with loose terms which could be construed as offensive. Stay up to date with issues like BAME—Black, Asian, and minority ethnic. When we first started at university there was a Gay Soc, which became LGBT, then LGBT+ and then LGBTQIA, which adds 'queer, intersex, and asexual' to lesbian, gay, bisexual, and transgender, which LGBT presents as an acronym. However, once again be aware what your 'clients' want. Then you have to make a choice on whether to work with them or not—and believe us, you will be asked to do some work you might personally find problematic (which of course you can refuse). Similarly first person pronouns, do

you identify as 'he', 'she', 'they', times change and you have to be aware and change with them.
- Politics—unless you are writing for a specific political party, ideology and so on, its best to stay politically neutral. Your client may ask for a particular 'leaning' but let them direct that. Don't just assume they share your own beliefs. You might be surprised how many of your own friends or family disagree with your political opinion. One again though, nobody can force you to take a job on if you feel you just can't stomach the point of view you are being asked to promote.
- Jargon—this is an odd one. Many think it makes their writing look on message, sharp and up to date. However, it dates very easily. How many people have you heard recently say, 'That's lush?' I can confirm my undergraduates said it a lot ten years ago, but it's been a long time since I heard it recently. Indeed, recently someone said, 'that's sick …' to me but I don't think they meant gruesome and 'cool' seems to have made a come back (but watch this space).
- Acronyms—don't expect your reader to know what NAWE is. Yes, it's the title of an organisation but if you are talking about it other than in NAWE journals you should say, NAWE (National Association of Writing in Education). Explain the acronym because your writing should not confuse the reader.
- Wordiness—we are writers, we like to use language in an evocative and provocative way, spin a good yarn, tell a tale and sometimes even show how smart we are. But clarity rests in simplicity. And we use the word clarity rather than perspicuity (say) but why didn't we just suggest, 'say it simple, say it clear'. You don't need the verbose, garrulous, loquaciousness of a writer like Will Self to talk about smart socks—even if you do respect him as a writer (which we do).

## 'Out of Work' Words

With limited word counts you have to decide which words work and which don't, but also which are redundant and have no job to do. Some are repetitions: that's 'tiny wee …' it's a huge big …', you get the idea. It's easy to get sucked into them. We all know the famous song about 'the bare necessities …'.

And there are the tautologies:

- Either it will rain tomorrow, or it won't rain.
- She is brave, or she is not brave.
- I will fall in love or I will not fall in love.

There are also the words which try to force the point being made. This is a very obvious mistake. It's a very useful idea. We very nearly managed it. Any clues here? It is very, very obvious. Do we need the word 'very'? It might be okay for the occasional flourish but be very careful with it.

Of course, it's really difficult to remember all the time. We really mean that. It's really worthwhile remembering, though. Which brings us to that other largely redundant word, 'really'. It is often really, really not worth including unless for effect.

There is or there are at the beginning of sentences are also out of work words. We recommend you think about framing sentences differently if you are tempted to use them:

- There are lots of ways to look at this problem.

Well, that is an okay sentence but it's also passive. Think about making it punchier:

- Look at the problem this way.

See how easy it is to make it more active by simply cutting there is or there?

There are lots of little things that we could look at in terms of grammar, like less or fewer, but this isn't a grammar book. Now work it out, could we have written that last sentence better? As we have said elsewhere, there are places to find this out.

## Muscular Verbs

You don't have to be a bodybuilder to know that the stronger you are the heavier the weight you can lift. Think about 'strength' when writing. Is the piece strong enough for the job in hand? It's a simple case of not just settling for the obvious. For example:

- Would the verb 'give' be better as 'donate' and would 'donate' benefit from becoming 'bequeath'?
- Would the verb 'say' be better as 'shout' and would 'shout' benefit from being 'scream'?
- Would the verb 'joke' serve better as an 'anecdote'?

In the end the advice is just don't settle for the first verb that comes to mind.

## Who, What, Not That, What Not

Working out when to use 'who', 'what' or 'that' is easy, but you will be surprised how often they are confused. We are the people *who* wrote this book—is correct. We are the people *that* wrote this book—is wrong. And if you write, 'We are the people *what* wrote this book'—you are in a wee bit trouble.

## Currently, Presently, Truly, Deeply—And Killing the—Lys and—Ings

Harry Kane is ~~currently~~ the captain of the England Football team. You don't have to write he is 'currently' the captain of the England Football team. The word currently is actually useless here because he either is or isn't the captain. But look out too for all the –lys in your copy then cut them, they said precisely. 'They said precisely' has no function here. Cut the –lys, we say. Adverbs are the bane of a copywriter's life—we say truly, deeply and sincerely (and now you can ask yourself do you care of we are delivering the message truly, deeply and sincerely when we have already written what you need to know?).

Similarly, words with '–ing' at the end require support when word counts are at a premium:

- She was walking.
- He was talking.
- They were dancing.

    Could be

- She walked.
- He talked.
- They danced.

Look out for examples of this, be alert to them, think about what they are 'saying' and when best to use or not use them.

'That' and 'which' are often interchanged but do you know which is which and why or what to use and when? Be alert to the possibilities. There is a good explanation here https://getitwriteonline.com/articles/which-vs-that/, but we can say that our preference is to use 'which' when a choice is available, for example:

- These are snazzy socks, which you will love.
- These are snazzy socks that you will love.

But it is worth having a look at the link (above); that's a fact, which you might find useful—which could be written, which is a fact that you might find useful. There is also something useful to be found in both of these sentences—any idea what it is? The use of a comma before 'which'—it's one of those small English grammar idiosyncrasies which I find interesting but see how it out loud, pausing on the comma and see how it breaks it up a little.

## Informal Contractions

That's a posh way of saying; one way to slim down the word count is to contract the words being used. 'The President is going to address the state of the country' is grammatically correct but we have moved into a century when we can say, 'The President's going to address the state of the country.' We can informalise the possessive 's':

- 'She is' can be 'She's'.
- 'It is' can be 'it's' and so on.
- Here are our snazzy socks becomes, 'Here's our snazzy socks.'

Not only does it contract the word count, it gives the delivery a more informal tone.

## Your Little Word and Phrase Tics

Finally, look for the words and phrases you might overuse. It's human nature to slip into an easy life and yet some simple tricks can turn an okay piece into a better one. Indeed (oops, sometimes we have a tendency to overuse that word) once you identify your own you can seek them out. We will scan this chapter for all the 'indeeds' and then filter them out as appropriate (or add them in). Mostly its common sense. Short, sharp sentences, sparkling prose, strong verbs, active deliver and confidence in what you are writing.

## Tools to Help with Editing

When it comes to editing, we can all do with someone else to look over our work. This isn't always feasible, but thankfully there are online tools that can help out. Which is the best? It's very much a personal choice, but we've listed a few below that we've found useful. Again, software and applications come and go very quickly, but do a google search on the top applications in the field you're interested in:

- **Spellchecker in Word**

    By all means, have it turned on, just don't rely on it!

- **Grammarly**

    We use this tool a lot and recommend it to our students. It's simple to use, and it comes with a free version. With any editing tool, it will make mistakes, but it's a good start. It comes in different versions including browser extension, mobile app, and a desktop application. With the free version, you can only edit a limited number of words—but you can copy and paste to get around this.

- **ProWritingAid**

    This is a pretty powerful tool—it looks for grammatical and punctuation mistakes, while also checking for structural issues such as repetition, clichés, and a lack of variety in sentence length. I've found this really useful for improving my writing, but it's rather detailed, so I tend to use it when I have more time and I want to find ways to improve my writing.

- **Ginger software**

    This application checks your text for spelling and helps fix the sentence structure. There's a basic free version.

- **WhiteSmoke**

    The company that provides this application describe it as having multiple systems to correct your writing, including grammar, punctuation and style.

- **Hemingway app**

    This is good at finding complex phrases. The online editing software checks for adverbs, spelling, and punctuation issues. The focus of this app isn't so much on picking up your typos, but to make your writing stronger. As they say, more 'bold and clear'.

## Key Chapter Points

- Professional writing means you will take a professional approach to delivering professional, high quality copy on behalf of someone else. This should not contain sloppy editing, loose phrases, lazy verbs, surplus to requirement adverbs and it *will* be 'active' as opposed to passive.
- Simple spelling and grammatical mistakes in writing can be costly, but as we show here, there is more to editing than running a spell and grammar check across your copy.
- When you're charging for copy, don't just bash it out and expect the client to edit it into shape. Repeat work comes from being able to deliver reliable, well-edited copy.
- There's a high demand for high-quality content. You need to ask yourself a very simple brace of questions. Does my work fit into that standard? If not, why not?
- Every business/client has a 'business style'. Not only does your copy have to correspond, if you can get it to make that style shine then you are more likely to get more work. So, think about the editing process as putting the icing and cherry on the already well-baked cake.

### Exercise 11.1
**This exercise is simple: take a pencil and edit this piece. Then have a look at the edit we did afterwards to see how much we agree, or not.**

The summer of 2018 is approaching, and Regent's Park Open Air Theatre in London has just announced that the highlight of their programme is *Peter Pan* by J.M. Barrie and an operetta of Henry James' *The Turn of the Screw*, music by Benjamin Britten and libretto by Myfanwy Piper. It says a great deal about the longevity of both of these fin de siècle stories that 200 years after they were written they still have a great deal to say about 'young people' and the stories that were written for and about them in the nineteenth century. We want to present this view of London to twenty-first-century visitors.

**Regent's Park Open Air Theatre** presents its summer 2018 programme. There are two major highlights:

- *The Turn of the Screw*—operetta (music by Benjamin Britten and libretto by Myfanwy Piper). A dark gothic tale of intrigue for warm summer nights.
- *Peter Pan*—story of the boy who didn't want to grow up. Will Captain Hook catch him this time? A timeless matinee for all the family.

Both performances say a great deal about our late Victorian history which is still relevant today. Get ready for two great theatrical events!

# 12

# Building a Successful Career as a Professional Writer

In this chapter we will consider:

1. What it takes to be successful when you're freelancing,
2. How to determine if you're ready to take the leap.
3. What it means to freelance, and can you make it work.
4. What to do if things go very wrong.

There's quite a lot to take on board when you first head down the path of freelancing. So, if you've been reading this book chronologically, then you might be feeling a bit overwhelmed. After all, being a freelancer seems to demand that you be a jack-of-all-trades. There are certainly lots of skills you need, but don't worry, many of these you'll quickly pick up the more you freelance, and as with most jobs, the more you do it, the more familiar the tasks become. For example, let's try chopping that sentence up—per Chap. 11:

> There are lots of skills you need. Don't worry, you'll quickly pick them up. The more you freelance the more familiar the tasks become. It gets easier, trust us.

See, what this tells you is that there are many ways to play around with the same text. The most important task is getting the message across.

Some embark on the freelancing journey through necessity and not choice. We know this. We are both writers with films, novels, poems, songs, articles, papers and chapter credits, all kinds of writing, under our belts. Writers often have jobs though. T.S. Eliot was a banker then an editor; Phillip Larkin was a librarian, Walter Scott was a lawyer, Bernardine Evaristo (novelist, Booker

Prize winner) is a university professor. But with the job market continuing to be ever more dynamic and evolving, it's not surprising that a lot more of us are working part time, or full time with a number of part-time roles. Landing a permanent position in this day and age is becoming ever more difficult. Nevertheless, sometimes freelancing is done through personal choice, and we want the flexibility that managing our own time can bring. Whatever your reason, if you're going to become a freelance professional writer, being successful at it will make it a whole lot easier. And that's what this chapter is about.

Up until now, we have discussed the skills and behaviours that help you get there. Now we're going to think about making this long term but also making it truly successful. When we say long term, it doesn't mean that you have to commit to freelancing long term. A lot of consultants we know jump in and out of freelancing, as the need arises. That's fine. But while it's good to be able to flex and adapt, it's also good to have a plan. This will give you focus and help you assess your needs and achieve your goals. I had written films and books but found myself at a loose end, which meant no money was coming in. So, I was able to do a little work to tide me over and have done so for the last 20 or so years. So, what we mean by successful is a question we can easily address. It means being in control of the destiny of your chosen vocation. Feeling that you are the captain of the ship, steering it in the direction you want to head, not simply being jostled about as the waves change direction. It means making enough from your writing to support your lifestyle.

## Understanding Your Skills and Capabilities

It's tempting to try and be everything to everyone, but this is rarely a good strategy. You might be able to get by, but it means that you don't build up any specialty. Initially, I addressed this by thinking about what I was interested in at the time. Being pregnant then as a young mother, helped me to identify magazines I could contribute to (and eventually edit). It's a good way in. I saw something I needed wasn't really there so I helped it along for others. Once my daughter went off to school I realised I wasn't best placed to be writing baby articles anymore—and so I moved on to other fields that were more aligned to my interests at that time, and wrote pieces regarding parenting older children, schooling and so on.

Standout freelancers are remembered. For example, I was recommended to a client by a satisfied customer, who described me as someone who 'listens and gets the job done'. It's a great recommendation and it's something you need to aspire to. Over time, I've come to see it as one of my strengths. I'm good at listening and making sure the client is aware that I've listened, and that I get the job done. It doesn't mean I'm perfect, because I have had projects that were delayed for lots of different reasons. Also, I've sometimes made mistakes with my estimating. But clearly the client didn't see me as the cause (usually it was due to factors outside my control, but regardless of the reason, clients don't always see it that way). What I do well, is communicate. If it looks like the work is expanding, I send of a short email to the client explaining that it looks like it's more work than we anticipated, and I give them a couple of options. They can choose not to do it, they can choose to do it and do it well, or we can do it but cut a few corners. What I do is put the client in the decision-making seat. And they like that. More often than not they go with the option that I think is best, but sometimes they don't—and when that happens the outcome is their decision.

> **Top Tip: How Would You Like Clients to Remember You?**
> Or if they were to recommend you to someone else, how would they describe you?

## Have a Niche or Two … or Three … or Four …

When you're responding on a project, often the client wants to feel they're getting someone who knows their field and understands what they want. If it's a website for Puppy Training, the last person they're going to hire is someone who has never owned a dog (or is uncomfortable around dogs—like one of us). They just won't get it. That doesn't mean that you have to be a puppy expert to get the gig, but you need to show that you are comfortable in their field. Therefore, if I can demonstrate that I've written for similar website in the past, perhaps on animal care, then there's a good chance I can deliver what they need.

A niche can mean many things. I know someone who's great at writing for make-up websites. But she specialises in affordable make-up brands. This means that she had to turn down a few gigs which were for up-market brands as it would have eroded her selling point (needless to say, like puppies this isn't my strength either—now guitars, well …). She has now quit her day job and focusses on writing blog posts about make-up products which companies send her to trial. They can see her past experience and that she's respected among her followers for providing honest, reliable reviews on affordable products. In turn, her followers know what products she'll be reviewing so the circle is squared—so to speak. But before reading on, think back to Chap. 11, you might like to consider how much information has been given in this chapter which you don't really need—the clue is in dogs, cosmetics and guitars. Did these interventions enhance the information given or just serve to entertain a little? In a book such as this, some small asides are okay because they break up the text, which can get a little dry in places. Were we writing this as a much shorter piece for a client we would be more careful, and would follow the mantra at the bottom of the previous paragraph: **deliver what they need**.

## Learn, Learn, Learn

One of the best tips we can give a freelancer is 'find out' and don't be afraid to 'learn'. Whether it's about researching and writing about a topic you know nothing about, or suddenly designing your own marketing poster. Give it a go. The Internet can be a great learning resource, with a lot of information and tools available—often for free. And if you use trusted sites here is so much good research you can do yourself, if you're prepared to put in the leg work and the time. Though we repeat 'trusted sites'. Be careful too, there are some which aren't so good, and you have to work at knowing the difference. Also, be careful about online offers which ask you to part with well-earned money. You shouldn't have to supplement this book with promises of earning £££££ or $$$$$ tomorrow. Bear in mind that is exactly what they are trying to do through their website. But much as we hate to say this, few lazy freelancers are successful. At best, they probably get by. This can-do attitude reflects well to clients—they generally like people who are prepared to try, roll up their sleeves, and learn.

Furthermore, it may not seem obvious at first, but a freelance writer also needs to be in tune with what's happening out in the world. Whether it's about blogging, content marketing, the latest webinars, the coolest social media platform—you need to stay informed. For example, as we write this, we are conscious of LGBTQ+, BLM and BAME issues (and if you don't know what these acronyms stand for look them up). As freelancers we have always been aware of our social and cultural responsibilities but as we write this, marches are taking place and public opinion is becoming polarised. This is where your network can help but watch the news, read the newspapers and stay up to date—all of which is easily accessed online.

## Be Realistic

It is pointless submitting articles if your writing just isn't up to scratch. And yes we know—this is a harsh reality you have to face. However, hopefully we have encouraged you to address issues and ideas to help you get better. Maybe it's your grammar, or perhaps your punctuation lets you down? What about you're formatting? Sentence structure? Formality of address? Informal writing style? These are basics and as professional writers, there is no margin for mistakes—you will be judged by the quality of every single piece of your writing. Even that email you wrote very quickly on your phone and didn't check—and predictive text is notorious for reforming the sense of your intended sentence. Today, while writing this, I sent a WhatsApp message to a friend which read, 'Bike tune done, early gray tea brewing ….' This should have been, 'Bike ride done, Earl Grey tea brewing ….' No harm done, of course, but 'Bike tune' made no sense and 'early gray' isn't 'Earl Grey' tea. Writing is your craft. So, hone it and keep honing it, check it for typos and sense, don't just rely on predict text and spell and grammar checkers. If you want clients to part with their cash for your services, they want it to be valuable.

Take a good hard look at your writing skills. Ask yourself, can you make them better? Is there anything you can do to improve? Well the obvious answer to this is in Chap. 11—practise, then practise some more. Then try to assess, am I ready? Is it good enough for someone to pay for your services?

> **Top Tip: Read, Read, Read**
> Keep reading those books on how to write, better writing, improving your writing. Join a writers' group and network with other writers. Don't neglect your editing skills and brush up on these from time to time. Read magazines with a pencil in your hand and edit as you read. Don't just let the words wash over you. Ask yourself, could I write that better? Or, why is that so good? It's your craft, so keep learning and keep polishing it until it gleams!

## Develop a Thick Skin

Yep, we won't deny it. Freelancing is not for the faint-hearted. Indeed, all writing is littered (literally) with rejection slips. You will meet unreasonable clients who will be unpleasant, unreasonable and downright rude. Our advice in these situations is to finish the job (if that's possible) and move on. Find other clients so you don't need to deal with them again. There's little point trying to win this argument (even if you are right), because they won't want to work with you again. Sure, you proved you were right—but at the expense of their ego, and they won't like you for it. So, grin and bear it, if you can. If not, forget it and move on.

> **Top Tip: Take It on the Chin, Smile, and Be Polite (It's up to You If You Want to Work with Them in Future Though)**
> It's always best not to end on bad terms—even if the client is completely unreasonable. You'd be surprised how small the world can be at times, and if it gets out that you're difficult to work with, it can take a lot of hard work and time to restore your reputation.

## Be Persistent

It will take time and success rarely happens overnight. But persistence will generally win, in the long run. Regardless of talent, if you can't handle rejection then you're not going to cut it as a freelancer. It's part of the job, and part of a writer's life. We will all be rejected for lots of different reasons, most of which we'll likely never know. If you get rejected, take a deep breath—go for a walk and get some fresh air if that helps—and then go back and send out another proposal.

## Become a Risk Taker

Is that job out of your league? It might be, then again … it just might be worth a shot. And what have you got to lose? If you want to develop and acquire new skills, then you'll need to push yourself out of your comfort zone. As unpleasant as it can be at times, it's good for you! Learn from it and out the learning to good use.

## Got to Really Want It

Freelancing is hard work, it can be lonely at times, and you're not going to be employee of the month anytime soon (unless you award it to yourself). But like most things in life, if you really want it, you'll need to focus on your goals. And you do need to be honest with yourself—if you've spent most of the month watching television on your couch, don't be surprised if your workload isn't what you want it to be. Which brings us to have long-term and short-term career plans. But before moving onto this, reel back a little. Actually, you can be the equivalent of 'employee of the month'. When something good does happen, and it will, stand back and give yourself a pat on the back. Learn from it, learn to do it again and again, but don't forget you are entitled to feel a little satisfied, at least.

## Having Long-Term and Short-Term Career Plans

Let's begin with the short-term plans. What do you need to get through the next few months? We give you a few examples:

- I need to have at least three to five writing gigs a month, so that I'm busy with paid work for at least three days a week.
- I'm going to focus on writing blogs for the retail industry, because I have some experience in that field.
- I'm going to be active on two freelancing websites, as I'm starting out and need to find some writing gigs. I'll aim to spend one day a week applying for projects.
- I've seen one or two local companies whose online presence could do with freshening up, so I'll contact them with suggestions.
- I'm going to teach myself how to use Excel so that I can manage my accounts better. Or even research top free accounting software options: https://blog.hubspot.com/sales/free-accounting-software (this site was written by a freelancer, just like you!).
- I've joined a local small business Facebook group—it's been really helpful in making contacts with other freelancers. I'm going to be more active, to see if I can generate some work through this channel. And so on.

The aim of these plans is to ensure, in the short term, that I can earn enough to make this a paying proposition. A freelancer I know used her short-term plan as a way to decide if she was ready to go full-time freelancing and give up her other job. She worked out what she'd need to make it viable—but also added the further requirement that she needed to be achieving those goals for 12 months before leaving her job.

Now let's think about some possible long-term plans:

- I really want to move into other fields. Travel is a real interest of mine. I'm hoping to do more travelling in the future, and I'd like to write about this. Therefore, I need to build up my writing skills in this area. I'm going to read up on travel writing, follow websites and blogs, such as the Lonely Planet, which publish good travel writing articles, and write some articles myself.
- I discover that travel writing is a pretty competitive field, so I want to have a few more options up my sleeve. I've just written a couple of articles for a

technology company that I found really interesting. I reckon this is a field I could do more in. I'm going to target technology companies and build up more examples in my portfolio. There's a technology conference coming up in a few months' time—I might pop along and see if I can make some contacts.

> **Tip:**
> conferences are held in hotels (usually—though many are now moving online). If you live in a hotel town or have hotels nearby and so on, check out what conferences they are hosting. You just never know who will be there. Distribute cards, leave flyers, get involved in conversations over coffee breaks (keep a spare lanyard with your name and details which you can slip around your neck, or a name tag you can pin to your shirt, they needn't know you have just walked in off the street),

- I'm good at writing blogs but I don't write much for other social media platforms. Given my blogging background, it would be a fairly easy transition. I'm going to follow other freelance writers on social media, see what they do online, and watch and learn. And so on.

These are all long-term goals of things we'd like to do in the future. It might not be achievable right now, but unless I make some steps to head in the right direction, I won't get there.

## When Things Go Wrong

Let's begin by saying, things will probably go wrong. That's okay! It's part and parcel of freelancing life (actually part and parcel of being a writer). So, what can you do when it does go wrong?

- Take a deep breath, don't feel sorry for yourself, brush yourself, and get back up again.
- Apologise (if you can) and show empathy. Yes, the client might have been in the wrong, but they had a bad day. They won't admit it, but it's better just to move on.
- If it's serious, get proper advice, and potentially consider consulting a solicitor, although it should never get to a point where such a huge mistake has been made.
- Learn from your mistakes. Look back at what went wrong? What steps would you take in future to avoid the same thing happening again? For example, was your agreement with the client water-tight or too vague? Did you have a plan? How was the communication on the project? If the client

> **Top Tip: Always Keep a Client's Business Confidential**
>
> Even if they are making material—copy and so on—public, that is up to them. Your relationship is strictly between the client and you, not the client and you and your next-door neighbour/best friend/lover/mother. I have heard other freelancers tell me things they shouldn't about a client's business. I don't mean things I should know (like what kind of person the client is, whether the business is legal and such like) but confidential, commercially sensitive matters, for example, which should remain confidential.

was difficult to get a hold of, what could you do differently in future to make it easier for them?

# Key Chapter Points

- Be brave and be prepared to take risks.
- Freelancing is a journey about constant learning—gaining new skills to meet dynamic needs—it's exciting, so embrace it.
- Things will go wrong—that's okay. Just have support ready. If you need support—such as with your business accounts or legal advice—make sure you get it.
- Be confident! Believing in yourself is so important when freelancing.
- Have a reputation for confidentiality.

**Exercise 12.1**
**What are your three biggest writing weaknesses?**
This exercise is about self-awareness of you as a writer. Knowing your weaknesses means you can work on improving them, and also be on the lookout for when they occur.

Be specific—is it your grammar? Do you make punctuation mistakes? Perhaps you type too quickly and leave typos in your wake (that's me!)? I know Andy's is overusing exclamation marks.

List your top three weaknesses as a writer.

**Exercise 12.2**
Write down three short-term goals and three long-term goals.

**Exercise 12.3**
Think about even the smallest issues that could be confidential and write a list, such as:

1. Addresses and telephone numbers
2. Your client's clients
3. Personal details of staff
4. A client's other businesses (I know someone who set a business up to rival his other successful business and became his own rival—because he knew if he didn't, someone else would. However, he made it out that both businesses were rivals and even kept it a secret, even from his staff (imagine if we found out Coke and Pepsi were the same and just pretending to be in competition?). I was writing for both businesses and had to keep up the pretence.)
5. How your client buys cheap and sells expensively.

# Appendix: LGA-Banned Words

The Local Government Association (LGA) in the United Kingdom has published a list of 200 words that all public sector bodies should avoid when talking to people about the work they do and the services they provide.

Included on the list of banned words are 'holistic governance', 'synergies', 'mainstreaming' and 'predictors of beaconicity'.

Some councils have already taken steps to ensure they use plain English. For example, 'civil enforcement officers' are now more traditional 'traffic wardens', and 'school crossing patrollers' have been replaced by 'lollipop men and women'.

The following is the list of the 200 words banned by the LGA:

Across-the-piece
Actioned
Advocate
Agencies
Ambassador
Area based
Area focused
Autonomous
Baseline
Beacon
Benchmarking
Best practice
Blue-sky thinking
Bottom-up

CAAs
'Can do' culture
Capabilities
Capacity
Capacity building
Cascading
Cautiously welcome
Challenge
Champion
Citizen empowerment
Client
Cohesive communities
Cohesiveness
Collaboration
Commissioning
Community engagement
Compact
Conditionality
Consensual
Contestability
Contextual
Core developments
Core Message
Core principles
Core Value
Coterminosity
Coterminous
Cross-cutting
Cross-fertilisation
Customer
Democratic legitimacy
Democratic mandate
Dialogue
Direction of travel
Distorts spending priorities
Double devolution
Downstream
Early win
Edge-fit
Embedded

Empowerment
Enabler
Engagement
Engaging users
Enhance
Evidence base
Exemplar
External challenge
Facilitate
Fast-track
Flex
Flexibilities and freedoms
Framework
Fulcrum
Functionality
Funding streams
Gateway review
Going forward
Good practice
Governance
Guidelines
Holistic
Holistic governance
Horizon scanning
Improvement levers
Incentivising
Income streams
Indicators
Initiative
Innovative capacity
Inspectorates
Interdepartmental
Interface
Iteration
Joined up
Joint working
LAAs
Level playing field
Lever
Leverage

# Appendix: LGA-Banned Words

Localities
Lowlights
MAAs
Mainstreaming
Management capacity
Meaningful consultation
Meaningful dialogue
Mechanisms
Menu of options
Multi-agency
Multidisciplinary
Municipalities
Network model
Normalising
Outcomes
Outcomes
Output
Outsourced
Overarching
Paradigm
Parameter
Participatory
Partnership working
Partnerships
Pathfinder
Peer challenge
Performance network
Place shaping
Pooled budgets
Pooled resources
Pooled risk
Populace
Potentialities
Practitioners
Predictors of beaconicity
Preventative services
Prioritization
Priority
Proactive
Process driven

## Appendix: LGA-Banned Words

Procure
Procurement
Promulgate
Proportionality
Protocol
Provider vehicles
Quantum
Quick hit
Quick win
Rationalisation
Rebaselining
Reconfigured
Resource allocation
Revenue streams
Risk based
Robust
Scaled-back
Scoping
Sector wise
Seedbed
Self-aggrandizement
Service users
Shared priority
Shell developments
Signpost
Single conversations
Single point of contact
Situational
Slippage
Social contracts
Social exclusion
Spatial
Stakeholder
Step change
Strategic
Strategic priorities
Streamlined
Sub-regional
Subsidiarity
Sustainable

Sustainable communities
Symposium
Synergies
Systematics
Taxonomy
Tested for soundness
Thematic
Thinking outside of the box
Third sector
Toolkit
Top-down
Trajectory
Tranche
Transactional
Transformational
Transparency
Upstream
Upward trend
Utilise
Value-added
Vision
Visionary
Welcome
Wellbeing
Worklessness
Source: http://news.bbc.co.uk/1/hi/uk_politics/7949077.stm

# Index

**A**

Audience, 10–12, 15, 22–28, 33–36, 70, 74–77, 79, 81, 83, 101, 145

**B**

Bid, 29, 87, 105, 113–125, 140, 146, 152
Bidding, 103, 104, 119
Bills, 3, 6, 9, 45, 124, 129, 130, 141, 143, 150, 151
Blog, 2, 13, 15, 20, 22, 26, 33, 37, 41, 48, 53, 71–73, 77, 85–88, 92, 95, 99, 101, 102, 105, 110, 112, 117–119, 131–133, 135, 138, 145, 152, 169, 173, 174
Brainstorm, 95, 147
Building network, 103, 105
Business style, 1, 14, 22, 166

**C**

Capabilities, 85, 91, 131, 168–173, 178
Career, 4, 6–8, 31–48, 83, 85, 88, 111, 127, 167–176
Casual, 6, 23, 30, 62, 64, 72, 123
Charities, 7, 15, 33, 35, 93–95, 111, 118, 119
Commitment, 48, 113, 123, 135, 142
Communication, 3, 4, 6, 10, 17, 18, 20–27, 34, 35, 49–67, 94, 106, 107, 115, 149, 153, 174
Competitive, 116, 139, 173
Confidential, 65, 175
Confidentiality, 94, 175
Craft, 6, 8, 11, 35, 48, 49, 84, 87, 147, 171
Creative, 3, 4, 6, 12, 24, 49, 66, 97, 109
Creative content, 33
Creative spark, 3, 4
Creative writers, 2–4, 7, 14, 49
Creative writing, 1, 2, 4–6, 11, 34, 38, 76, 89, 133
Critical, 4, 9–11, 50
Customer relationships, 97, 106–107
Customers, 1, 14, 15, 18, 20, 22–24, 26, 27, 35, 39, 50, 51, 63, 70, 71, 84, 85, 88, 97–101, 105, 107, 111, 112, 118, 121, 123, 124, 145, 156, 157, 168, 178
CV, 35, 74, 90, 97, 98, 105, 108–112, 116

## D

Deadline, 27, 32, 46, 106, 107, 109, 119, 123, 144, 147, 148, 150, 151
Decision-making, 169
Design, 1, 18, 19, 35–37, 72, 91, 93, 100
Digital, 22, 37, 69
 era, 14
 media, 70–72
 platforms, 73–74
Documents, 2, 21, 28, 36, 52, 53, 65, 91, 106, 107, 109, 121, 123, 124, 150
Drafting, 40, 146

## E

Elevator pitch, 99, 111, 112
Emails, 10, 18, 21, 24, 26, 28, 34, 35, 38, 44, 46, 47, 49, 50, 52, 53, 55, 58–66, 77, 80, 86, 99, 101, 106, 109, 111, 123, 136, 145, 147, 155, 156, 169, 171
Energy, 4, 143
Estimating, 127–140, 146, 149–151, 169

## F

Feature articles, 92, 133
Finessing, 8, 66
Focus, 27, 38, 41, 46, 47, 87–91, 104, 108–111, 116–118, 144, 154, 158, 165, 168, 172, 173
Formal, 30, 53, 59, 60, 64, 72, 123, 136
Formatting, 64, 79, 109, 121, 171
Forums, 13, 85, 87, 95
Freelance, 7, 8, 10, 11, 14, 20, 22, 23, 28, 33, 36, 38–47, 50–52, 65, 83–85, 87, 88, 90–92, 97, 102–106, 108, 111, 112, 114, 127, 128, 130, 137, 139, 140, 143, 167, 168, 170, 174

## G

Goals, 17, 34, 38, 52, 57, 63, 100, 168, 172, 174, 175

## H

Hours, 13, 23, 31, 39, 43, 44, 51, 64, 65, 70, 71, 78, 86, 94, 98, 105, 106, 113, 116, 121, 128–133, 136, 137, 139–142
House style, 11, 94

## I

Images, 2, 11, 12, 14, 15, 18, 20, 22–28, 30, 34, 36, 47, 54, 56, 65, 69, 71, 72, 75, 78, 79, 85, 88, 147, 149, 155
Impact, 10, 21, 22, 27, 70, 71, 77, 78, 103, 107, 124, 131, 135
Informal, 6, 12, 60, 62, 157, 164, 171
Interviews, 85, 95, 146, 148

## K

Keeping track, 147–148

## L

Language, 7, 9, 10, 12, 14, 15, 17, 19, 22–26, 30, 36, 37, 53, 55, 58, 60, 64, 66, 72, 76, 111, 115, 161
Learn, 35, 63, 77, 88, 95, 98, 127, 136, 155, 170–174
Letters, 17, 20, 26, 59, 81, 94, 155
Listener, 48, 50, 84, 111
Listening, 4, 65, 169
Long-term career, 172–174

## M

Managing, 41, 141–152, 168
Manuals, 37, 150

Marketing, 13, 20, 34–36, 42, 58, 84, 92, 148, 170
Markets, 18, 21–26, 36, 37, 42, 47, 54, 55, 69–83, 105, 127, 139, 145, 149, 152, 168
Media, 13, 20, 22, 23, 26, 33, 36, 39, 42, 43, 70–74, 83, 85, 86, 90, 99, 101, 102, 104, 108, 134, 151, 152, 158, 170, 174
Mistakes, 9, 10, 14, 18, 19, 22, 27, 28, 36, 46, 47, 51, 59, 101, 102, 105, 136, 147, 151, 162, 165, 166, 169, 171, 174, 175
Money, 2, 4, 5, 7, 17, 23, 24, 33, 34, 42, 45, 66, 77, 83, 93, 98, 99, 111, 114, 120, 128, 136, 140, 168, 170
Multimedia, 92
Multiple projects, 44, 151

N

Negotiating, 18, 128–130, 136, 137, 139
Niche, 34, 48, 76, 101, 102, 104, 106, 112, 134, 139, 169–170

O

Objective, 22, 24–25, 27, 28, 40, 52, 53, 57, 58, 86, 122
Online, 8, 12, 14, 22, 23, 26–29, 33, 34, 37–40, 42, 46, 54, 69–83, 85, 90, 95, 97, 99, 103, 104, 106–108, 110, 145, 146, 152, 164, 165, 170, 173, 174
Online sources, 101–105
Opportunities, 8, 21, 35, 71, 87, 93, 101, 107, 111–116, 121, 122, 124, 152

P

Paid, 3, 14, 32, 34, 38, 43, 44, 86, 92–94, 102, 104, 105, 135, 137, 155, 173
Patience, 46, 50, 84
Paying career, 31
Pitching, 40, 41, 101, 104
Planning, 128, 130, 141–152
Platform, 13, 22, 38, 73–74, 83, 86, 88–90, 102, 103, 113–125, 133, 140, 149, 170, 174
Portfolios, 8, 39, 47, 83, 85, 89–93, 95, 98, 102, 104, 114, 119, 120, 124, 174
Press, 34, 36, 47, 73, 92, 93, 158
Price, 17, 36, 71, 115, 120, 121, 128, 131–133, 136, 137, 157
Pricing, 36, 131–137
Product, 8, 13–15, 18, 22, 23, 27, 32, 33, 36, 41, 54, 63, 65, 71, 76, 77, 84, 116, 121, 145, 148, 149, 156, 157, 169, 170
Profession, 6–8, 31–33
Project management, 148–151
Promotion, 34, 36, 145
Proposals, 11, 14, 18, 21, 22, 27, 35, 36, 44, 51, 60, 103, 113, 114, 116–125, 136, 172
Protocol, 94

Q

Quality, 1, 6–8, 10, 11, 14, 32–34, 37, 50, 56, 57, 71, 72, 78, 84, 85, 91, 95, 101, 103, 107, 114, 125, 131–133, 136, 166, 171
Questions, 6, 10, 27, 28, 41, 45, 46, 50, 51, 53, 59, 62, 76, 79, 85, 87, 91, 103, 111, 112, 114, 115, 118–120, 125, 127, 134, 144, 152, 158, 159, 166, 168

**R**

Rate, 1, 6, 43, 47, 77, 99, 104, 105, 114, 116, 127, 130, 132–141
Read, 2, 7, 20, 25, 32, 35, 59, 60, 69, 70, 74–78, 103, 114–118, 120, 124, 147, 154–156, 158–160, 170, 171, 173
Reader, 6, 24–30, 36, 37, 41, 52, 53, 58, 59, 61, 64, 65, 69–72, 74–80, 102, 122, 141, 143, 147, 160, 161
References, 21, 61, 66, 78, 98, 101, 113, 146, 155
Relationships, 1, 18, 26, 49, 50, 55, 62, 66, 100, 101, 106–107, 112, 147, 148, 175
Reports, 2, 13, 18, 21, 22, 49, 53, 58, 61, 77, 85, 87, 110
Reputation, 14, 21, 28, 52, 93, 102, 134, 135, 142, 172, 175
Research, 12, 32, 34, 41, 53, 67, 73, 74, 92, 95, 99, 101, 102, 104, 119, 122, 131, 133, 134, 137, 139, 140, 142, 144, 145, 147–150, 152, 170, 173
Risk, 21, 141, 143, 151, 172, 175

**S**

Sensitive, 59, 175
Sentence structure, 25–26, 54, 165, 171
Short-term career, 173–174
Skills, 4, 5, 8–11, 18, 20, 22, 27, 28, 32–34, 36–38, 40, 41, 45, 49, 65, 66, 84, 89–91, 93, 95, 98, 100, 101, 105, 109–111, 114, 116–118, 120, 124, 125, 131, 134, 138, 139, 167–173, 175
Sources, 17, 35, 79, 97–105
Strengths and weaknesses, 87
Style guide, 11, 27, 72–73, 80

Subject, 12, 22, 24–25, 28, 32, 34, 37, 44, 56, 61, 63, 64, 79, 85, 86, 88, 91, 93, 95, 102, 112, 136, 147, 158

**T**

Targets, 15, 18, 22, 24, 25, 35, 36, 45, 55, 73, 76, 79, 115, 145, 154, 174
Techniques, 8, 37, 54, 63, 87
Things go wrong, 174–175
Time, 3, 21, 33, 50, 70, 83, 98, 114, 128, 141, 154, 168
Time management, 109
Tone, 12, 15, 17, 22–26, 30, 41, 53, 56, 58, 60, 72, 79, 123, 156, 164
Topic, 12, 32, 36, 53, 61, 75–78, 92, 110, 115–118, 147, 152, 154, 170

**U**

Unpaid, 136, 141
Updates, 40, 45, 46, 71, 92, 106, 123, 124, 150

**V**

Vague, 64, 114, 119, 138, 145, 174
Volunteering, 93–95

**W**

Weaknesses, 87, 175
Website, 4, 11, 13, 14, 23–26, 29, 33, 34, 37, 38, 41, 49–52, 65, 67, 70, 71, 73, 74, 77–80, 83–87, 89, 91, 95, 97, 99–104, 106, 108, 110, 112, 117–119, 129, 130, 135, 137, 138, 142, 145–147, 152, 169, 170, 173
Word choice, 15, 25–26, 77
Work independently, 84

The manufacturer's authorised representative in the EU is Springer Nature Customer Service Centre GmbH, Europaplatz 3, 69115 Heidelberg, Germany. If you have any concerns regarding our products, please contact ProductSafety@springernature.com

Printed and bound by CPI Group (UK) Ltd, Croydon, CR0 4YY

23/03/2026

02076747-0013